THE CANADIAN GENERAL ELECTION OF 1984

Politicians, Parties, Press and Polls

By Alan Frizzell
Anthony Westell

With contributions by Nick Hills, Jeffrey Simpson, and Val Sears

Carleton University Press
Ottawa, Canada

©Carleton University Press Inc., 1985

ISBN 0-88629-036-8

Printed and bound in Canada

Canadian Cataloguing in Publication Data

Frizzell, Alan Stewart, 1947-
  The Canadian general election of 1984

ISBN 0-88629-036-8

1. Canada. Parliament — Elections, 1984.
2. Mass media — Politial aspects — Canada.
3. Canada — Politics and government — 1984-
I. Westell, Anthony, 1926- II. Title.

FC625.F75 1985/ 324.971'0647   C85-090268-1

Distributed by: *5̄2, 931*
  Oxford University Press Canada
  70 Wynford Drive
  DON MILLS, Ontario, Canada M3C 1J9
  (416) 441-2941

ACKNOWLEDGEMENT

Carleton University Press gratefully acknowledges the support extended to its publishing programme by the Canada Council and the Ontario Arts Council.

THE
CANADIAN GENERAL ELECTION
OF 1984

Politicians, Parties, Press and Polls

CARLETON CONTEMPORARIES

A series of books designed to stimulate informed discussion of current and controversial issues in Canada and to improve the two-way flow of ideas between people and government.

PREFACE

This book is intended to be the first in a series, one to be published after each Canadian general election. The purpose is to present in concise and readable form a record of the election and an analysis of the results. We hope that this and each succeeding volume will be of interest in itself, and that the series will make a contribution to the history of politics in Canada.

As Co-directors of the Carleton Journalism Poll surveying public opinion on political and other issues for the news media, we have tried to bring the precision of social science research methods to the aid of journalism. In this book also we seek to marry the two approaches to the examination of public affairs. The first chapter, in which we set the stage for the election, is journalistic in its recording and interpretation of events, and to report and discuss the campaigns of the major parties, we have enlisted three distinguished journalists who were active in the coverage of the election. However, the chapter on media coverage is social science — indeed, probably the largest content analysis of its kind carried out in Canada. The analysis of the vote in which we draw on the work of political scientists also is social science. We have to declare an interest when we write on the role of polls during the election, and when we use data from the national election polls we conducted for Southam News to support our interpretation of the results.

Six Research Assistants at the Carleton University School of Journalism gave us valuable help with this book: Jeff Abbott, Michael Martin, Angela Patten, Miriam Rautiainen, Steve Ritz, and Michael Way.

Ottawa
August, 1985

Alan Frizzell
Anthony Westell

CONTENTS

CHAPTER 1

SETTING THE STAGE

The five year period preceding the election of 1984 was perhaps the most extraordinary in the political history of Canada. There were two general elections and three Prime Ministers. The economy staggered through the worst recession in half a century. A referendum in Quebec challenged the very existence of Confederation. The federal government forced through the patriation and reform of the constitution, making fundamental changes in the political system. The proclamation of a National Energy Policy outraged and further alienated much of Western Canada. There was a crisis of sorts in relations with the United States. And on top of all this there was at least the normal quota of political alarums and excursions arising from the clash of an ambitious Government and a determined Opposition which resorted at one point to the unprecedented tactic of refusing to assemble for a vote in the House of Commons so that the House was effectively prevented from meeting for days on end.

When John Turner became leader of the Liberal party and Prime Minister, he tried to detach himself from the events of the past and to direct the attention of the voters to the future. But the record was surely in the minds of the voters when they went to the polls in 1984, and it probably played a large part in persuading many to choose the Progressive Conservatives to form the next government. That is not necessarily to say that the Liberal record was all bad; in fact it included substantial achievements. But any government eventually wears out its welcome, and after years of turmoil, some voters may simply have become tired of high-pressure politics, crises and confrontations. In voting for change, they were perhaps in some measure voting for a quieter national life. However that may be, to understand the mood of the election, it is necessary to review briefly the extraordinary events of the recent past.

THE CONSERVATIVES

By 1979, the Liberals had been in power for 16 years, and Pierre Trudeau had been a controversial Prime Minister for 11 of them. The country was ready for a change, and to win the election on February 18 it was mainly necessary for the Conservative campaign to keep out of trouble, and in particular to avoid as far as possible close scrutiny of the leader, Joe Clark, who even then was regarded as something of a political liability. The surprise was not that the Conservatives won, but that they actually polled fewer votes than the Liberals and elected only 136 MPs, against 114 for the Liberals, 26 for the New Democratic Party and 6 for the Creditistes in Quebec. Clark could form therefore only a minority government, but it soon became apparent that he suffered from the sin often laid to Trudeau, arrogance. He made clear that he intended to govern as if he had a majority, and this led him to defeat after only 259 days in power. The Conservative government's budget introduced on December 11 was widely regarded as a responsible attempt to reduce the deficit, but the higher taxes were not popular, particularly the additional duty of 18 cents a gallon on gasoline. Warned that the Liberals and New Democrats might vote together to defeat the budget and force an election, Clark did nothing. He could not apparently believe that the Liberals, having recently been beaten, would dare to face another election, and he was confident that if they did, the voters would take the opportunity to return his government with a majority. He was wrong on both counts. The budget was defeated, and in the following election on February 18, 1980, the Conservatives suffered a major defeat. The Liberals won 44 per cent of the vote and 146 seats (shortly raised to 147 by a special election in the constituency of Frontenac). The Conservatives obtained only 32 per cent of the vote and 103 seats. The NDP won 20 per cent of the vote and 32 seats.

This remarkable political reversal in nine months led not only to the return of Trudeau at the head of a strong government, about which more later, but also to the downfall of Clark as Conservative leader. The principal concern of the voters in the election seemed to have been national leadership. They clearly preferred Trudeau, with all his warts, to Clark who had been tagged by the Toronto Star with the derisory nickname of Joe Who when he emerged from relative obscurity to win the party leadership in 1976, and who had been cruelly labelled a wimp by his critics. His defeat now opened the way for enemies in his own party to question his leadership. The most active enemies were those on the right wing of the party who thought Clark was too far to the left of centre — a so-called Red Tory — but there were many others willing to lend a hand in bringing him down. Some doubted his ability ever again to lead the party to victory; others were ambitious to succeed him; a few no doubt were continuing the old feuds that had wracked the party for years. Their opportunity came at the party's national convention in Ottawa in 1981 when the delegates were required by the constitution to vote on whether or not they wanted a leadership convention. Sixty-six per cent wanted no convention, thereby registering confidence in Clark; 34 per cent voted for a convention, implying that they wanted to get rid of Clark, or at least were so uncertain about his leadership that they were willing to see it tested in a race against other candidates. Clark at once acknowledged that, as a vote of confidence, this was not good enough, and he pledged himself to do better at the next national conference in two years' time.

Back in the House of Commons, he performed creditably as Opposition Leader and seemed to be maturing as a politician and a personality. But his enemies within the party, and even within his parliamentary caucus, were relentless in organizing his downfall. When the next party conference came around, in Winnipeg, in January 1983, there was another vote on whether or not to hold a leadership convention. Clark improved his support only fractionally; there were still some 33 per cent voting for a convention — against him, as it were. He decided on the spot that he could not continue to lead the party toward the next election if the feuding and division continued, and that it was time to face his enemies. He announced that he would resign as leader, thus forcing a leadership convention, but that he would also be a candidate to succeed himself.

Then began a race for the leadership in which eventually there were eight candidates. Clark led throughout, but he was closely pursued by Brian Mulroney. Mulroney had worked for years in the backrooms of the party and was a well-known and liked figure in Quebec, but he had never stood for election to the Commons, or for any other public office. He was thought, probably wrongly, to be to the right of Clark in the Tory spectrum, and this was important because many of the most active party members were shifting their opinions to the right, following in some measure the lead of President Reagan in the United States and Prime Minister Thatcher in Britain. He had the advantages also of being fluently bilingual and of coming from Quebec where the Conservative party needed to find new support and win more seats if it was ever to become a truly national party and secure election as a majority government. There was perhaps among the delegates to the leadership convention in Ottawa on June 11, 1983, the feeling that they would appear rather foolish if, after going through all the turmoil of the past three years, they merely re-elected Clark as leader. Clark had been tried and had failed to keep the party in power; Mulroney seemed to offer at least the prospect of a brighter future for the party. On the fourth ballot, Mulroney was chosen leader: 1,584 votes to Clark's 1,325.

The Conservative party had its new beginning, and Mulroney, soon securing a seat in the Commons, took his place as Leader of the Opposition and began to show his skills as a political leader. He demonstrated the talent for friendship and conciliation for which he was known in Quebec and which the feuding Tories badly needed. But he also began to promise the country a new style of politics to contrast with the confrontational methods of Prime Minister Trudeau.

PIERRE TRUDEAU AND THE LIBERAL GOVERNMENT

Following the defeat of the Liberals in 1979, Trudeau had announced in November his intention to resign as leader. But within a few weeks, the Conservative government had blundered into defeat on the budget and the country was heading into another election. Trudeau saw the opportunity to regain power and readily accepted an invitation from his party to withdraw his resignation and to lead it in one more campaign. With Clark and the Conservatives well behind in the opinion polls, it was now the time for Trudeau to stay out of trouble and let the voters defeat the government. He ran on the whole a bland campaign but there were a couple of important policy statements pressed upon him by his closest advisers who tended to be to the left of the centre of the party and, by inclination, Canadian nationalists. So Trudeau promised to broaden the mandate of the Foreign Investment Review Agency and also, as part of a new energy policy, to increase to 50 per cent the level of Canadian ownership in the oil and gas industry. His private agenda, however, as it became clear later, was to strengthen the position of the federal government in Canada. It was ironic that having entered federal politics in 1965 to defend the federal power against the attacks of Quebec nationalists and separatists, he had in fact presided as Prime Minister over a massive transfer of spending power to the provinces. Also, by inviting the provincial premiers to repeated summit meetings to discuss national affairs, often before the television cameras, he had raised the premiers to a level of national importance they had never before enjoyed. They came to be seen as the legitimate spokesmen for their provinces on issues of national policy, bypassing Parliament. By 1980, Trudeau had decided that the decentralization of power had gone too far. He was determined to stop the erosion, and if possible to recover some power for Ottawa. The scene was set therefore for confrontation, and for Trudeau, in his last years of power, to secure his place in history.

The first challenge and opportunity were awaiting Trudeau when he returned to office. The Parti Quebecois government was asking in a referendum for a mandate to negotiate Sovereignty-Association with the rest of Canada. This was thought to be a clever tactic because Quebeckers were not being asked to make the big leap to independence, but merely to see if it would be possible to arrange to have at the same time political sovereignty and economic association with Canada. Nevertheless, it was clear that a Yes vote in the referendum would be a first step toward separation and independence. This was the battle for which Trudeau and his federalist colleagues had been waiting. At last they could engage head-on the separatists and nationalists against whom they had been warning Quebeckers for years. They plunged into the referendum debate, and one of their weapons was to promise that if Quebeckers would reject Sovereignty-Association, they would guarantee reform of the Canadian constitution to meed the legitimate concerns of the province. It is questionable if this promise had much influence on the vote — the average Quebecker was probably more concerned about a job, pension rights and other economic benefits associated with Confederation than with the constitution — but it certainly committed the federal Government in Ottawa. Quebeckers voted No by roughly 60-40 per cent in the referendum on May 20, 1980, and Trudeau the next day set about reforming the Canadian constitution. One crisis had passed with the defeat of the challenge to Confederation posed by the Parti Quebecois; now another was at hand.

The British North America Act had been passed by the British Parliament in 1867 to create the Canadian Confederation, and it remained under the control of

Westminster because federal and provincial governments had never been able to agree on an amending formula — that is to say, on how they would make changes in the constitution once it had been patriated, or brought from Britain to Canada. To patriate and make major changes in the constitution, therefore, it was first necessary to win agreement on an amending formula. Trudeau himself had for years been ambivalent about seeking reform of the constitution. He thought it would strengthen national unity if Canadians could agree on a set of values and express them in a charter of rights, which would certainly include the rights of the French and English languages, to be entrenched in the constitution. On the other hand, he had warned that to open the constitution for amendment might be to open, in his phrase, a can of worms, and he was satisfied that Quebec had under the BNA Act all the powers it needed to flourish within Canada. After a long series of negotiations with the provinces had ended in failure in 1971, Trudeau shrugged off the issue of constitutional change. But in 1980, after the referendum, it was again top priority. Justice Minister Jean Chretien toured the provinces to sound out their ideas, and in June Trudeau met the premiers in Ottawa to work out an agenda. But a full-scale federal-provincial summit in the fall, held in a fierce glare of publicity, ended in bitter failure. With the enthusiastic encouragement of their parliamentary caucus, Trudeau and his Cabinet decided to proceed unilaterally — that is, to seek the patriation and reform of the constitution without the consent of the provinces. They would ask Parliament to approve a package providing for patriation to cut the last colonial tie to Britain, for an entrenchment of a Charter of Rights and Freedoms, and for an amending formula.

The reaction was explosive. Ontario and New Brunswick saw merit in the federal proposals, but the other eight provinces were outraged by what they saw as the arrogance of Ottawa's unilateral action to change the constitution over their objections. In the Commons, Clark led the Conservative opposition in opposing the government's resolution, deploying both argument and the familiar weapon of filibuster. The NDP leader, Ed Broadbent, split his own party by supporting the government plan in return for improvements he requested; New Democrats in the West in particular were unwilling to support almost anything sponsored by the unpopular, indeed hated, Trudeau. The courts were drawn in when the provinces rushed to ask for rulings that the federal Government had no right to proceed without their consent. The Supreme Court of Canada hardly clarified the issue when it ruled that while there was no *legal* reason why the federal Government should not act unilaterally, it would be *constitutionally* improper because custom and practice required at least a measure of provincial support. But the question then arose of whether the British Parliament would accede to a request from Ottawa for patriation against the wishes of a majority of the provinces.

There were, however, other forces at work in the situation. Trudeau and his team knew from their polling of public opinion that the idea of a Charter of Rights was appealing to Canadians , and this became manifest when the draft Charter was referred to a parliamentary committee for scrutiny. Witnesses queued up to express their approval in general and to argue for specific changes. The committee listened and redrafted, and the proceedings became an impressive exercise in participatory democracy. Although the Government had to some extent lost control over the contents of its Charter, it was also clear that it had powerful public support. This put pressure on the premiers — by now known as the Gang of Eight — while on the other hand, Trudeau wanted if at all possible to avoid a showdown at Westminster where the ambiguous ruling of the Supreme Court might cause all sorts of problems. Both sides agreed to try once more for agreement. The summit conference convened in Ottawa on November 2, and in four days of dealing and wheeling, the full story of which remains to be discovered and told, the federal Government and nine of the provinces arrived at an agreement, acceptable to all but fully satisfactory to none. Only Quebec refused to sign. Within the month, Parliament approved the package with only a handful of MPs opposed. In March, 1982, the British Parliament gave its consent, and on April 17 Queen Elizabeth proclaimed the new constitution in a ceremony on Parliament Hill. "And No One Cheered," as Keith Banting and Richard Simeon later titled their book of commentary on the implications of the new constitution. But then, Canadians are not demonstrative people, and while they might have taken quiet satisfaction from the fact that the constitution was at last home in Ottawa, and included a charter of rights, the long struggle had probably exhausted their patience. Trudeau had achieved many of his goals, but at the price of embittering most of the provincial premiers and confirming his reputation as a Prime Minister who preferred confrontation to cooperation, and who was obsessed with constitutional issues when he ought to have been dealing with bread and butter problems such as unemployment. As for the new constitution itself, it remained to be seen how it would work. The amending formula imposed on Trudeau by the premiers against his better judgement appeared to be so rigid that although the constitution was at last under Canadian control, it might not be possible in future to make changes in the balance of federal and provincial powers. By entrenching rights and freedoms, the Charter had put them effectively beyond the control of Parliament, thereby curtailing the supremacy of Parliament, a doctrine that had been at the heart of parliamentary democracy. Interpretation of the charter rested with the courts which would in the future have to play a much larger role in policy-making than had been the custom in Canada.

ENERGY

The National Energy Policy announced in October 1980 sprang from the oil crises of the 1970s. The previous Liberal government had been engaged in a long struggle with Alberta, and to a lesser extent with Saskatchewan and British Columbia, to keep a lid on prices in Canada as they soared in world markets, and to obtain a larger share of the revenues that flowed from higher prices. The brief Conservative government had also had its share of problems with Alberta and never quite obtained a pricing agreement. The new Government decided on a bolder approach: it would not merely settle the energy issue, but use it also as the basis for an industrial strategy and as a way to assert the power of the national

government. The paper announcing the NEP began with the challenging statement: "This is a set of national decisions by the Government of Canada. The
decisions relate to energy. They will impinge, however, on almost every sphere of
Canadian activity, on the fortunes of every Canadian, and on the economic and
social structure of the nation for years to come. They have major, positive
implications for the federation itself." The policy went on to make wholesale
changes in the way in which oil and gas prices were fixed; in the way in which
revenues were to be shared between the federal and provincial governments and
the companies; and in the system of taxing oil and gas companies and offering
subsidies to steer development. The federal Government declared also that it was
"committed to a significant shift in the structure of the oil and gas industry. It has
three goals: At least 50 per cent Canadian ownership of oil and gas production
by 1990; Canadian control of a significant number of the larger oil and gas firms;
an early increase in the share of the oil and gas sector owned by the Government
of Canada."

The NEP therefore was a red rag to the oil-producing provinces which saw the
federal Government moving in to control their resources; to the business community which saw that the strategy was not merely to increase Canadian ownership in the industry, but also to expand the public sector by a process of
nationalizing private companies; and to the multinational oil companies, most
of them American, because their subsidiaries in Canada were threatened by the
policies on pricing, taxation, regulation and Canadian ownership. There was of
course bitter resistance in the House of Commons where the Conservative
opposition was dominated by Western members.

The NEP was clearly based on the belief that oil prices would continue to rise.
In fact, they were softening as the world economy slowed, new sources of energy
were developed, and demand for oil eased. Even without the NEP, the extraordinary boom in Alberta brought about by soaring oil prices would soon have
been over. But unfortunately for the federal Government the introduction of the
NEP and the end of the boom more or less coincided, and Ottawa got the blame
when exploration slowed down and drilling rigs moved south by the dozen
because prices were higher in the United States and the prospect of profits
greater. There is much that could be said in defence of the NEP, and the program
was popular with nationalists and, at least initially and in a general way, with the
voting public. But the political impact in the end was certainly negative for the
Liberal Government. The West was further alienated. The business community
was concerned by what it saw as the socialistic ideas inherent in the NEP.
Political and media opinion leaders in the United States were disturbed by the
Government's nationalism.

CRISIS IN RELATIONS WITH THE UNITED STATES

Within weeks of the announcement of the National Energy Policy in Canada,
Ronald Reagan was elected President of the United States with a mandate to
restore U.S. prestige abroad and to reduce the role of government at home. He

was well disposed toward Canada and had in fact proposed what he called a North American Accord to establish closer cooperation between the United States, Canada and Mexico. But his government team lacked experience in managing the relationship with Canada, and the neo-conservative philosophy was directly opposed to the interventionist mood of the Trudeau government. While the Reaganauts believed in less government regulation and intervention in the marketplace, the Trudeau team was planning more intervention and public ownership. While Washington wanted to ensure the free flow of U.S. trade and investment abroad, Ottawa was discriminating against U.S. investment in Canada. The U.S. Government was not so crass as to argue that Canada could not do as it wished with its own energy industry, even to the point of nationalizing U.S.-owned oil companies if it paid fair compensation. It did, however, object to some aspects of the NEP which it thought to be unfair to U.S. investors — in particular, the so-called back-in provision under which Petro-Canada, or some other state agency, could claim a 25 per cent interest in any oil or gas discovery on federal territory. The U.S. Government, speaking on behalf of U.S. companies, regarded this as no better than expropriation of private property, although it could be argued from the Canadian side that the Government, by tax incentives and grants, was paying a major share of the exploration costs. The U.S. Government was concerned also by Ottawa's plan to expand the powers of the Foreign Investment Review Agency, which it saw as a barrier to U.S. investment in Canada and as an arm of government which, in defiance of GATT trading rules, imposed conditions on U.S. corporations wishing to do business in Canada. The attitude of the new U.S. Government toward Canada was not improved when President Reagan visited Ottawa early in his term and was met by noisy crowds demonstrating against U.S. policies, and by a Prime Minister who was courteous but clearly not much in sympathy with the right-wing ideas of his guest.

Diplomatic exchanges over these and many other bilateral issues — for example, acid rain — became increasingly irritated in tone and it was possible without much exaggeration to write in 1981 of a crisis in the Canada-U.S. relationship. One interpretation, popular among Canadian nationalists, was that the two countries were set on divergent courses toward different national goals, but this overlooked the fact that the Liberal Government, with its interventionist and nationalist ideas, was a political accident rather than a true reflection of the wishes of the Canadian people; it was in office only because the Conservative Government under Clark had proved even less attractive to the voters. The real mood in Canada was probably more conservative than activist, and beginning to look with interest at the Reagan model of neo-conservatism. In any event, the idea of a confrontation with the United States was not popular in the Liberal Cabinet where the cautious moderates were again beginning to tame the nationalists and interventionists. The NEP was modified to meet some U.S. objections, and the plan to expand FIRA was dropped. U.S. spokesmen went out of their way to insist that there was no crisis and that in fact relations between the two governments were good, and by 1982 the crisis was over. By the following year, the Liberal Government was even proposing to discuss sectoral free trade with the United States. But the suspicion remained that Trudeau and his advisers had endangered the vital relationship with the United States, and might do so again. The Conservatives began to say that in order to ensure good relations, it would be necessary to defeat the Liberals and elect them, a plank that became increasingly important in their political platform.

THE ECONOMY

The state of the economy as revealed by the level of unemployment, the rate of inflation, or by some other measure apparent to the public, is a major issue in almost every general election, and sometimes the decisive issue. In 1984 it was even more important than usual because the country was only just emerging from a harrowing recession, and because of the pervasive and uneasy fear that the foundations of the system were threatened by changes in technology that nobody quite understood. The popular belief that Liberal governments were, if nothing else, good managers had been eroded by bad times, and the Conservatives seemed more confident than their adversaries in their claims to know how to improve the situation. In retrospect, the Liberal success in overthrowing the Conservatives and returning to power in 1980 may be seen as a dreadful political mistake, for in 1981 the Canadian economy was caught up in the world-wide recession about which the Government could do relatively little. Had the Liberals remained in opposition, the Conservative Government would have had to deal with the recession as best it could, and the Liberals could have produced again the old slogan that "Tory Times are Hard Times", and could probably have won in 1984. As it was, the Tories escaped the storm, and the Liberals paid the penalty.

Economists will no doubt continue to argue about the roots of the worst world recession since the 1930s, but for present purposes it is enough to identify the second oil shock of higher prices administered by the OPEC (oil exporting) countries in 1979-1980. Fearful of another round of rapid inflation, the OECD (major industrial oil importing) countries agreed in the Spring of 1980 to tighten their fiscal and monetary policies in order to restrain growth and so deter a sudden rise in prices. Perhaps because the developed industrial countries were acting together for the first time, these austerity policies were all too successful in preventing inflation. As Sylvia Ostry, who was chief economist at OECD headquarters in Paris, put it later in a speech delivered at Carleton University, the rate of inflation fell and energy efficiency increased, but, "Instead of a brief transition to renewed growth the industrialized countries suffered the worst recession since the Second World War. Growth slowed throughout the area while unemployment rose grimly and steadily. Signs of severe financial strain became evident as company balance sheets sharply deteriorated. Bankruptcies in every OECD country reached record levels. The debt position of many Second and Third World countries became increasingly precarious and interest rates rose. The (U.S.) dollar rose, commodity prices plummeted and export markets shrank. Protectionist pressures were fanned by rising unemployment and exchange rate distortions, especially the overvalued (U.S.) dollar and the undervalued Yen."

Canada, depending heavily on primary industries and on exports, suffered all these ills and more. The economy turned down in the third quarter of 1981 and experienced six straight quarters of decline. Output fell, unemployment rose, profits went down, incomes shrank, bankruptcies in businesses and on the farms climbed, interest rates soared above 20 per cent at one point. All this was traumatic for a country that had grown comfortably accustomed to economic growth and prosperity, and that had been led to believe that any government that knew its business could readily fix whatever went wrong in the growth machine. The Liberal Government, far from giving an impression of knowing what it was doing, often seemed to be simply confused. It tried a variety of tactics in a succession of budgets, relying at one stage on a program of resource-based megaprojects to stimulate the economy, at another on a program of wage restraints, and then on make-work schemes to hire the unemployed. The recession ended early in 1983, and by the end of the year, output was about back to where it had been in 1981 when the trouble started. But unemployment remained high; it was still 11 per cent when the election was called in 1984. And there was a new phenomenon to worry the voters — the budget deficit. The Trudeau governments had tended to spend more than they taxed even during the prosperous years, but when the recession cut into revenues and forced more social spending, the deficit climbed rapidly, to a forecasted $31.5 billion in 1983-4. Experts might argue over the economic implications, but in the minds of many voters, the deficit and the accumulated national debt became symbols of Liberal extravagance and incompetence.

As if the recession itself were not enough, the country began to understand in the early 1980s that vast and menacing changes were occurring in the world economy. Companies in newly developing countries were rising to challenge many of the old smokestack industries on which the developed world had relied for work and wealth. To earn their way, it was said, the developed countries would have to shift from an industrial to a post-industrial economy, producing information and services rather than goods. In the process, millions would have to change jobs, even lifestyles. And nobody was quite sure how to bring about the necessary changes, if in fact they were possible at all. For Canada in particular, with its small market and relatively inefficient manufacturing sector, the problems seemed almost unsurmountable. At the very least, it must have seemed to many voters, it would take a new government with new ideas to clean up the economic mess and make a plan for the future.

THE NEW DEMOCRATS

If times were tough for the Liberals, they were hardly better for the New Democratic Party, as Nick Hills describes in detail in the following chapter. Ed Broadbent's support for the Government's constitutional initiatives had split the party, and at the national convention in Regina in 1983 there was even a plot to remove him as leader, but it soon fizzled. More seriously, Jim Laxer, formerly a prominent left-winger, resigned as the party's Research Director and circulated a paper analysing and criticizing some of the party's basic policy positions. He argued that the NDP was stuck with the economic ideas and goals of the 1950s and 1960s while reality was changing rapidly. His criticisms were resented by some sections of the party and rebutted by others, but his diagnosis reflected what seemed to be a widely-held opinion: the NDP was going nowhere and had little to contribute to the real debate on economic issues. As attention focused on the new Conservative leader, Mulroney, and on the race for the leadership of the Liberal party, the NDP sank in the polls, and it appeared to be in danger of losing its place as a significant party both inside and outside Parliament.

CHANGE OF LEADER

Trudeau's last hurrah was the peace initiative he launched late in 1983. Concerned by the deteriorating relations between the two super-powers, the United States and the Soviet Union, he set out to try to bring them to the bargaining table by mobilizing the pressure of world opinion. Travelling to Washington, Western and Eastern Europe, India, China and to other countries to meet national leaders, he sought to inject political energy into the situation — specifically, to bring about a conference of the five nuclear powers. His mission reflected growing world concern over a drift toward nuclear war and was popular with the Canadian public. But it never seemed likely to succeed because the real initiative obviously rested with the super-powers. The best that could be said about Trudeau's initiative was that it was worth trying in a dangerous situation. The worst that could be said by his enemies was that it was a desperate attempt to regain popularity, and indeed the polls did show an improvement in the popularity of the Liberal Government. But that was probably of no great concern to Trudeau because he had said he did not intend to run in the next election.

As 1984 opened, the announcement of his retirement was eagerly awaited by the news media, and of course by all those Canadians who had come to see him as the author of the country's problems. He chose February 29, Leap Year day, to inform Liberal party president Iona Campagnolo of his wish to retire as leader and to request that a convention be held to choose his successor. He told journalists who caught him leaving his office that evening that the previous night he had been out walking in a blizzard: "I went to see if there were any signs of my destiny in the sky. There weren't, there were just snowflakes." Having slept on it and done some judo in the morning, he called Campagnolo to tell her his decision. Whether it really happened that way, or whether Trudeau was wrapping himself in the cloak of romance and mystery with which he liked to intrigue the public, we may never know. But his decision began officially the leadership race that had long been anticipated.

JOHN TURNER

Far behind the Conservative party in the polls, and facing the unknown qualities of Brian Mulroney, the Liberal party was looking for a leader who would be a winner. The members of the Trudeau Cabinet were tarred by the unpopularity of the Government, and John Turner seemed an obvious choice. He had entered the House of Commons in 1962, been appointed to the Pearson Cabinet in 1965, made a stylish run at the leadership in 1968, and then served in the Trudeau Cabinets as Justice minister and as Finance minister. The reason for his sudden resignation as Finance minister in 1976 had never been convincingly explained: some said he could no longer serve with Trudeau because of clashes of personality and differences on policy, and others said that with Trudeau firmly occupying the office of prime minister, Turner's ambition was frustrated and he decided to go into private life and make his fortune in corporate law. There were a few even who felt that Turner deserted the Government in difficult economic times rather than take hard and unpopular decisions. Whatever Turner's real motive, and probably he had a mixture of motives, the fact that he had distanced himself from the Trudeau Government was no liability when that Government fell into times of unpopularity. Turner then began to appear as the heir apparent to the leadership, or as the shining knight who could be relied upon to take over the leadership and save the party in its darkest hour. Although Turner played very little part in politics between 1976 and 1984, the news media maintained their interest, and that of the public, in his potential. He seemed to have about him a touch of political magic, and this remained even after Trudeau announced his first resignation in 1979 and Turner declined to run. At that time, apparently, he decided to put his young family and his law practice first. By 1984, he was still ambivalent, according to his biographer, Jack Cahill. In his book, *John Turner — The Long Run*, Cahill said that when Trudeau announced his plans to retire, Turner was in Jamaica on holiday. He had not even discussed running with his wife, and he had forbidden eager friends to build a shadow organization. After eight years in private life, he worried that his political skills had become rusty, and he was concerned that he would not be able to live up to the expectations created by the media. None of this was apparent to the kingmakers in the Liberal party or to the news media. It was simply assumed that Turner could have the leadership more or less for the asking, and could then trounce the inexperienced Mulroney in an election campaign. In the event, Turner proved to be a better judge of his capabilities than his supporters and admirers. He announced in Ottawa on March 16 that he would seek the leadership, and it was soon apparent that he was having trouble making the return to the rough and tumble of politics.

He stumbled over policy, fumbled relations with the new breed of adversarial journalists, and found himself in a real race with Jean Chretien, perhaps the ablest campaigner in the Trudeau Cabinet and the most attractive of the flock of ministers who sought the leadership. There was never much doubt that Turner would win a majority of the delegates' votes, but Chretien was busy winning hearts with his emotional appeals to patriotism and the Trudeau coalition. At the Ottawa convention on June 16, Turner won on only the second ballot, with 1,862 delegate votes against 1,368 for Chretien. It was not by any means a famous victory. The campaign had rubbed some of the shine off the knight's armour. Chretien and his supporters were bitterly disappointed; Canadians in general had probably preferred Chretien as a fighting politician to Turner who seemed to be inheriting the leadership of the party and the prime ministership as if by right. Although the publicity attending the leadership race had given the Liberals a lead in the Gallup Poll, the expectations that Turner had feared were already in danger of turning sour in the mouths of the voters.

Trudeau resigned as Prime Minister on June 30, and immediately Turner and his Cabinet were sworn in. With no new talent available, Turner was forced in the main to recycle Trudeau's Cabinet which had been widely written off by journalists eager for change as one of the weakest since Confederation. To present at least the image of freshness, Prime Minister Turner reorganized and simplified the elaborate Cabinet bureaucracy created in the Trudeau era, but the gesture created little impression. The question now was whether Turner would call an early election or wait until the fall. It is probably fair to say that most outside observers expected him to decide for delay so that he could take firm control of the Government, announce some new policies, recruit new candidates and put the Liberal party machine in order before facing the voters. But inside the Liberal caucus, the almost unanimous opinion was to go the country at once on the momentum of the leadership race and while the polls were favorable. Nothing was likely to improve by the fall, and much could go wrong, said the Liberal MPs and Senators — with the conspicuous exception of the new Deputy Prime Minister, Jean Chretien, a wily politician who wanted Turner to spend the summer months impressing himself upon the country as prime minister so that he could carry that prestige into a fall campaign against the untried Brian Mulroney. Turner listened to the majority and on July 9 announced that the election would be on September 4. He explained: "Any government to take the kind of steps required by current economic circumstances needs a clear and fresh mandate." With the departure of Trudeau, one of the most controversial leaders in Canadian history, an era was ending. In the final five years at least, it had been an era of active government and fiercely partisan opposition in which drama followed drama in the theatre of national politics. Both Turner and Mulroney were promising a new style of government and of politics, without being specific. This campaign would be more important than usual in influencing the voters.

CHAPTER 2

THE CAMPAIGN

THE VINCIBLE LIBERALS

by Jeffrey Simpson

Mr. Simpson writes the daily political column from Ottawa appearing on the editorial page of The Globe and Mail. He is the author of *Discipline of Power*, a prize-winning account of the rise and fall of the Conservative Government in 1979-1980.

The Liberal Party, which had dominated Canadian politics throughout the twentieth century, suffered the worst defeat in its history in the September 4 election. What had been perceived as a scarcely vincible political party was revealed in the campaign to have been a magnificent illusion, a party short of money, organization, effective leadership, ideas and ultimately of votes. From 147 seats in the 1980 election, the Liberal Party tumbled to 40 seats. Its share of the popular vote dropped from 44 per cent to 28 per cent, a humiliation as overwhelming as it was unforseen by those Liberals, including leader John Turner and most of his Cabinet, who rushed into an election when prudence —and the counsel of Jean Chretien — dictated a delay of at least until the fall of 1984.

Murphy himself could have formulated his law from the Liberal campaign. Seldom, if ever, in Canadian political history has a major party conducted a campaign of such sustained ineptitude. From a complete misreading of public opinion on the eve of the campaign, Turner proceeded to spend the first two weeks of the campaign without proper travel arrangements and adequate staff; to perform indifferently in three nationally televised debates; to fail to identify and articulate salient themes in his campaign; to be observed tapping female derrières, and to refuse to apologize quickly for what many people considered an insulting gesture; to change campaign managers, styles and tactics in mid-election; to authorize mindless negative advertising of the kind he had vowed never to countenance; in short to campaign without verve, consistent direction or imagination. The result of this sustained ineptitude, coupled with the party's weaknesses masked by the magnificent illusions of its last years in power, reduced the Liberals to small clusters of MPs from Atlantic Canada, Quebec and Ontario, and two lonely and widely separated MPs from Western Canada —Lloyd Axworthy in Winnipeg and Turner himself in Vancouver.

The search for adequate explanations for the debacle must go beyond the campaign itself. Inevitably, the search must begin with the 16 years in office of Prime Minister Pierre Trudeau. And even then, the search may not be directed sufficiently backwards in time, for if there was one overriding reason for the Liberal debacle, it was a deep, almost desperate, desire for a change of government. Liberal, Conservative and public polls before and after the campaign confirmed this knawing desire. And who can say what precise mixture it was of Trudeau's 1980-1984 term, his scarcely unbroken 16 years in office, or the Liberals' near-hegemony in federal politics from 1963 to 1984 that so preyed upon the voters' perceptions that they chose decisively not merely to defeat the Liberals but to humiliate them.

Pierre Trudeau, whatever his undeniable achievements, never paid careful attention to the organization and structure of the Liberal Party. Occasionally, he summoned an interest in party affairs, usually upon finding himself in political difficulty. But such matters as financing, headquarters staffing and funding, candidate recruitment, rank-and-file motivation, and polling never received his persistent attention. Instead, he delegated these matters to a handful of close advisers and colleagues, men such as Marc Lalonde, Keith Davey, Jim Coutts and Tom Axworthy. Since they all worked either for or in close proximity to him — and derived their power from him instead of from positions in the party or caucus — they were free, indeed encouraged, by him to re-make the party organization as they saw fit. This inevitably meant aggrandizing their own power, and by definition his, at the expense of the party in the country, in caucus or even in Cabinet. When Trudeau finally retired, he turned over a campaign organization centred in his own office. Although the Trudeaucrats subsequently reproached Turner for spurning their talents, his attitude, however politically unwise in the circumstances of an early election, was easily explained by his misgivings about what the Trudeau men had wrought by their disregard of the Liberal Party organization. It was the bitterest irony of the Liberal campaign that Turner, having dispensed with their services at the beginning of the campaign, turned in the desperate days of mid-campaign to the very Trudeaucrats whose ways he had denounced and publicly decried. By campaign's end, Turner had Davey as campaign director, Axworthy as policy adviser, and former

Trudeau officials Michael Kirby, Michael Gillan and Gordon Ashworth, among others, running his campaign. The Liberal advertising executives in Red Leaf Communications who had worked for Trudeau directed a television, radio and newspaper advertising campaign that was as ineffective as its negative advertisements were insulting.

Turner later claimed that although he had realized that the Liberal Party organization had been allowed to wither, he had never fully appreciated the extent of the atrophy. His perceptions can be debated, but there was little doubt that the Liberals lagged behind the Conservatives in such organizational ingredients as polling sophistication, direct-mail advertising, candidate training, media relations, and tour planning. Not only had the Conservatives devoted more time to these tools of modern politics and campaigning, they had the money to pay for them. In 1983, the Conservatives raised $14-million ($4-million through their leadership review), compared to $8-million for the New Democrats and $6-million for the Liberals. No wonder that when Bill Lee, Turner's ill-fated first campaign manager, arrived at Liberal headquarters to begin the campaign, he found the offices under-staffed and ill-equipped. Liberal headquarters, like so many other parts of the Liberals' magnificent illusion, looked impressive to an outsider but could not respond to a severe challenge.

Another Trudeau legacy was the weakening of the party in all four Western provinces. This enfeeblement had been proceeding apace since John Diefenbaker wrested a majority of Western seats from the Liberals in the late 1950s, and while occasionally checked, as during Trudeaumania in 1968, it was never reversed. At his departure, Trudeau had pushed the Liberals to below 25 per cent of popular support in the four Western provinces. When Turner spoke of restoring the Liberals as a "national party", he meant in part improving its credibility in Western Canada. He put his own parliamentary career on the line by running in Vancouver Quadra.

Turner also had something rather more fundamental in mind in speaking about restoring the Liberals as a national party. He had entered politics in 1962 as MP for a Montreal constituency, and witnessed the modest electoral successes of the Pearson Liberals in the 1963 and 1965 elections. He received his first Cabinet appointment from Pearson, being sworn in on the same day as two other new ministers, Chretien and Trudeau. For Turner, the Liberal Party of the Pearson era was the one he admired far beyond what the party became under Trudeau. The Pearson coalition, roughly speaking, was that of Mackenzie King and Louis St. Laurent minus the Western support siphoned off by Diefenbaker. The Liberals retained good links with the business community. The party's support remained solid in French Canada, among immigrants, and across all income groups.

Trudeau's 16 years in office altered that coalition by deepening the Liberals' appeal to some groups and the disaffection among others. French Canada rallied ever more strongly to Trudeau, giving his party 74 of 75 seats in the 1980 election. Similarly, the party's appeal grew among many so-called ethnic Canadians, especially from Mediterranean countries and the Indian sub-continent. And in the 1980-1984 period, the Liberals systematically set out to attract more low- and moderate-income voters in order to squeeze the New Democrats, a strategic decision by a handful of Trudeau advisers who felt that the party's 1979 defeat had been caused by insufficiently differentiating the Liberals from the Conservatives. Liberal polls also showed the party under Trudeau to be more popular than its rivals among women and first-time voters. Yet Trudeau drove away from the Liberal Party voters — and sources of finance — on whom the Pearsonian party had depended. The steady enfeeblement of the party in Western Canada has already been noted. So, too, the business community's relations with the Trudeau Liberals were often frosty. Although businessmen directed many reproaches at Trudeau, the most severe were those involving the National Energy Program, the Foreign Investment Review Agency and Finance Minister Allan MacEachen's ill-fated 1981 budget. It was little wonder that the Conservatives were so successful in raising money from the business community in the year preceding the election. More broadly, the Liberals' polls showed a steady deterioration of support among upper middle-class families in English Canada, especially Ontario, the "two-car families in suburbia" as Tom Axworthy described them. The narrower but deeper base which had sustained Trudeau was not to Turner's liking. He preferred the wider, shallower base of the Pearsonian Liberals because such a party could call itself truly "national", and in good electoral times could win handsomely in all regions of the country rather than, in effect, conceding so many seats, especially in Western Canada, before the election began. Of course, the reverse of Turner's hopes for a wider, shallower coalition of voters also held true; in bad electoral times, a party without unshakeable loyalties in certain narrow linguistic, regional or socio-economic groups risked being decimated.

Relations between Trudeau and Turner were cordial, but never close, during the years of their Cabinet association. The two men not only had quite different personalities and backgrounds, they saw Canada and its problems in different ways. These different perceptions, which were compounded by personal relations that grew distant and even frosty after Turner's departure from Cabinet, contributed to the intellectual confusion and political contradictions of the Liberal campaign. Put boldly, Turner during his years of exile had become increasingly disillusioned with Trudeau's governments. His praise was limited to bilingualism and to certain social policies. His private criticisms were extensive: a) Trudeau demoralized and politicized the public service; b) Trudeau excessively centralized power in his office and the Privy Council Office, thus weakening traditionally strong departments and their ministers; c) Trudeau completely disregarded party organization, including candidate recruitment, and relied excessively on his small group of political advisers; d) Trudeau believed in a centralized form of federalism which provoked needless confrontations with provincial governments; e) Trudeau ran a fiscally imprudent government which relied too much on deficit financing and piled up $150-billion in public debt; f) Trudeau unnecessarily impaired relations with Canada's NATO allies and the United States; g) Trudeau pursued erratic economic policies, including excessive government intervention in the economy which weakened domestic and foreign investor confidence, and an energy policy which sought the twin goals of self-sufficiency and greater Canadian ownership in the wrong ways. In short, there was little Turner applauded in the Trudeau performance, and his applause grew distinctly fainter after years of mingling with business circles skeptical of, if not downright hostile to, Trudeau's government.

Turner could say none of these things publicly without risking a messy row with Trudeau. So touchy were relations that when Turner told reporters during his leadership campaign that he had left politics in 1975 because Trudeau would not support efforts to achieve voluntary wage-and-price controls, Trudeau promptly issued a press release disputing Turner's version of events. Fearful of a public row, Turner retreated into an elaborate code for getting across his message that much of the Trudeau legacy needed to be overhauled or jettisoned. He steadfastly refused, for example, from the moment of his first press conference as leadership candidate, to discuss government decisions from 1975 to 1984. But his leadership campaign themes made clear what he thought of Trudeau's stewardship: a reduction in the deficit and public debt; improved federal-provincial relations; better communications with the United States; greater appreciation of Western Canadian concerns; a re-organization of the Liberal Party; traditional Liberal policies of progress on issues of special importance to women, universality of social programs and improved retraining schemes. The only two major Trudeau initiatives Turner pledged to continue were federal bilingualism and a reduction in the nuclear arms race.

The trouble was that many Liberals found Turner's themes either distasteful or undesirable. Thousands of Liberals who admired Trudeau as a person or for his policies, or both, viewed Turner's inclinations with dismay. And in Quebec, where Trudeau remained the province's most respected figure, implicit criticism of him was bound to harm Turner's standing. Thus Turner soon discovered that the Trudeau legacy was a millstone for his own purposes of changing the party to his own liking, and an electoral advantage among those voters who remained wedded to the agenda and orientation of Trudeau. Compounding Turner's dilemma was a problem of political tactics he was unable to resolve. In altering the composition of the Liberal coalition, Trudeau had designed policies that some left-of-centre voters might find attractive, especially in such policy areas as social programs, nuclear disarmament, and energy, and they served the political purpose of squeezing the NDP. For a year prior to Trudeau's departure, the NDP hovered at 10-12 per cent of the popular vote, down from the 18 per cent it had won in the 1980 election. Turner's implicit criticism of Trudeau policies, coupled with his own career as a Bay Street lawyer and the public image this had created for him, left the Liberals tarnished in the eyes of so-called "marginally committed" voters who could swing between the Liberals and the NDP. Certainly until mid-election campaign when he changed advisers, tactics and strategy, Turner was prepared to countenance an erosion of this kind of support in exchange for improving the party's fortunes among small-c conservative voters. But what ultimately happened was what Turner both created an opening which the NDP exploited brilliantly, and failed to make inroads into the Tory vote.

The unravelling of the Turner mystique began at his press conference opening his leadership campaign. He immediately found himself on the defensive for his views on the Manitoba language question and on the federal role in protecting minority language rights. In response to an all-party resolution in the Commons urging approval of a language rights package negotiated by the Manitoba

Government and the province's French-language spokesmen, Turner declared:

"On the Manitoba question, I support the spirit of the parliamentary resolution, but I think we have to recognize that what is at issue here is a provincial initiative, and that a solution will have to be provincial. And, I would hope that it would be resolved by the political process and not by the judicial process."

He repeated this view, using many of the same phrases, in subsequent television interviews on *The Journal* and *Canada AM*. Those repetitions eliminated any doubt that he had inadvertently mis-stated his position. Indeed, the position had been carefully refined by Turner, his adviser and friend John Payne, and others in his campaign to send a signal to Western Canadians that the Liberals would be more flexible in linguistic matters and that the party no longer held Trudeau's fixed belief that linguistic policy represented the key to national unity.

The French-language press immediately picked up Turner's remarks. Editorialists and other commentators denounced him both for misunderstanding the Manitoba language question and for implicitly rejecting the Trudeau Government's long-standing commitment to use federal constitutional power, if necessary, to protect minority-language rights. Within days, the issue had spread to the English-language media. Naturally, his statements alarmed his Quebec supporters who urgently sought meetings with Turner to repair the damage in their province where Conservative leader Brian Mulroney quickly picked up the issue. Turner, under intense pressure from Quebec, soon issued a "clarification", a word that subsequently took on a life of its own as symptomatic of his mis-statements of policy. His "clarification" read: "There is no doubt in my mind that such fundamental minority-language rights must, if abused, be remedied by the judicial system and that the federal Government has the duty at times to intervene, either in Manitoba or in Quebec or elsewhere."

Turner drew a distinction between minority-language rights, which might require federal intervention, and provincial responsibility for the extension of minority-language services. Although Turner subsequently won about half of the Quebec delegates at the leadership convention, he did so because a majority of them believed that he was the only candidate who could carry the country. But the language question took the shine from his mystique as a decisive, resolute leader.

Seven candidates entered the race to succeed Trudeau, but only Turner and Chretien were conceded any chance of winning. The other five — Donald Johnston, John Roberts, John Munro, Mark MacGuigan and Eugene Whelan — presented themselves for the also-rans' usual mixture of motives, their lack of national stature offering eloquent testimony to the indifferent front-bench talent surrounding Trudeau. None of them even got to play kingmaker, although MacGuigan tried by crossing to Turner by pre-arrangement after the first ballot. But the switch meant nothing; Turner needed only 125 more votes after the first ballot and he would have collected them whatever MacGuigan did. The first ballot results were: Turner 1,593; Chretien 1,067; Johnston 278; Roberts 185; MacGuigan 135; Munro 93; Whelan 84. The first-ballot results clearly showed that Turner could not be prevented from winning on the second: Turner 1,862; Chretien 1,368; with Johnston clinging to 192 votes.

It was a misleading triumph that sent false signals to Turner, his advisers and the Liberal Party. Early in the leadership campaign, a cliché took hold in the media that Turner would win delegate votes but Chretien would win their hearts, and like many clichés this one contained an element of truth. On the night of his victory, Turner admitted as much to the delegates, calling Chretien the most popular man in the party. Moments earlier, party president Iona Campagnolo had hailed Chretien as the "man who came in second but first in our hearts". Chretien had conducted a more energetic, pleasing campaign than Turner. The Liberal Party organized five regional all-candidates' meetings, and Chretien performed better than Turner at at least three of them, and possibly four. Whereas Turner seemed incapable of tearing himself from carefully scripted answers written on filing cards, Chretien spiced his replies with wit and partisan jabs at the Conservatives. Whereas Turner tried to put distance between himself and the Trudeau record, Chretien unashamedly defended the substance of that record while promising to run a more accessible, open government. Chretien portrayed himself as a true small-l liberal, disagreeing for example with Turner's priority of deficit reduction. Chretien called himself proudly the candidate from Main Street, contrasting his roots with his rival's Bay Street career. He urged delegates to vote with their emotions and to keep fighting for liberal principles. He even quoted St. Exupery: "One only sees clearly through the heart". His supporters were devoted to him, and rare was the Liberal anywhere who could find anything nasty to say about him, except in the Quebec Liberal caucus where powerful Quebec ministers Andre Ouellet and Marc Lalonde dismissed their colleague as an intellectual lightweight.

Lalonde and Ouellet were typical of Liberal Party powerbrokers across the country. In almost every province (Newfoundland and British Columbia being exceptions), the party establishment, defined as the ex-officio delegates to the convention (Cabinet Ministers, MPs, MPPs, Senators, federal and provincial executive members), overwhelmingly preferred Turner as the candidate who could pull the party from its low standing in the polls. Turner and Chretien roughly split the delegates elected at the constituency level, who accounted for about two-thirds of the total. But Turner was reckoned to have carried the approximately 1,000 ex-officio delegates by a margin of about three-to-one, enough to secure his victory. This represented the greatest, and the ultimately the most tragic, irony of the Liberal demise; the establishment, whose members were by definition most closely associated with the Trudeau legacy, voted massively for the candidate most eager to repudiate that legacy, solely because it was thought he could bring victory again to what had been the western world's most successful national political party. Seldom, if ever, has Canadian politics witnessed a more monumental miscalculation.

The false signals sent out by the Turner victory continued in the aftermath of his convention triumph. The Liberal Party had reached the pre-election nadir in its popularity in 1983, and then climbed slowly in the winter of 1983-1984, thanks to marginally improved economic conditions and to Trudeau's peace initiative. The party still trailed the Conservatives badly when the leadership campaign began. Naturally, the national media focused its political coverage almost exclusively on the leadership campaign, all but ignoring the Conservatives and New Democrats. The result of this disproportionate coverage was a steady improvement in Liberal fortunes as many formerly disaffected Liberals returned to their traditional home. By the end of the campaign, the Liberals had inched ahead of the Conservatives in public polls. One such poll showed the Liberals leading by a heady nine points, but a survey taken by Liberal pollster Martin Goldfarb immediately after the convention put the Liberals ahead 46 per cent to 42 per cent. These polls led Turner into two grievous miscalculations. The first was to call an early election; the second to begin his campaign in a leisurely, almost indifferent, fashion.

Within days, even hours, of the convention, an overwhelming consensus grew among senior Liberals that Turner should go for an early election to capitalize on the momentum of the leadership campaign. Among Cabinet ministers, only Chretien and Doug Frith demurred. They counselled that by delaying the election until autumn, Turner could accompany the Queen and the Pope on their scheduled Canadian tours, undertake several international trips, present a budget or an economic statement to the House — in short, control the political agenda and show his prime ministerial stuff to the country. John Payne, Turner's close friend, also advised caution. But the rest of his advisers either prevaricated or urged a speedy election call, and Turner, whose instincts had previously led him to favor delay, yielded to the prevailing wisdom around him. In so doing, he misread the significance of the polls, believing them to confirm the Liberals' restoration and his own popularity rather than to be the result of the disproportionate publicity the Liberals had received, a situation to be rectified in an election campaign.

So, too, the polls induced a studied over-confidence in the Turner camp, an over-confidence made the more remarkable by the lamentable lack of preparation by the Liberal Party organization. Turner, having called the early election, seemed disinclined to campaign right away. Naturally, he was tired from his leadership campaign, from the exertions of forming a government, and also from a whirlwind trip to Britain to ask the Queen to postpone her summer trip. No sooner had the campaign begun than the Tories committed two gaffes. The first involved a memorandum by an assistant to Tory finance critic John Crosbie estimating the cost of the party's election promises as $6-billion. The second involved jocular remarks about patronage made by Mulroney aboard his campaign plane. These gaffes merely confirmed Turner's belief that the old Tory penchant for self-destruction was again at work. In addition, these early Conservative stumbles offered Turner further evidence that his principal adversary was a lightweight who could be counted upon to make mistakes under the pressure of his first election campaign. As a result, Turner had to be cajoled by his aides into campaigning in the first two weeks, and it showed. His performances were indifferent, his speeches lacked substance, and the organization of his tour was poor. While the other leaders flew around the country in chartered jets with staff and reporters aboard, Turner moved by commercial airplanes and reporters scrambled to catch up.

It revealed much about the state of the Liberal campaign organization and Turner's own lack of preparation that confusion surrounded even the appointment of national campaign co-chairmen. It had been agreed before Turner's quick trip to England to see the Queen that Lise St. Martin Tremblay, Doug

Frith and Izzy Asper would be co-chairmen — all fresh faces. Turner had agreed to phone Marc Lalonde to tell him that the Quebec position on the campaign committee would not be his, and promptly forgot. As a result, on the night before the election writ was issued, Turner learned that Lalonde was already busy, acting on the presumption that he would again run the Liberal campaign in Quebec. That put St. Martin Tremblay off the committee, which in turn meant a campaign committee without women. In the panic, Judy Erola was pressed into service as a chairperson, but only as he was driving to the committee's opening press conference did word reach Frith on his car telephone that he would not be a member. Similarly, Turner struck seven policy committees chaired by Cabinet ministers. Their work dribbled out throughout the campaign, usually not in time to help desperate Liberal candidates looking for material in the first month of the campaign.

From the beginning of the election campaign, Turner tried to portray himself as the candidate of change. "I have not been part of the administration for the past nine years," he told his first press conference of the campaign, "and I do bring a new face and a new policy to the government." That certainly reflected Turner's own self-image, and it jibed with what one of his pollsters, Angus Reid of Winnipeg, was advising him (but not with the advice from Goldfarb, a Trudeau loyalist). The obvious difficulty was that this theme of change could not easily be squared with the Cabinet Turner selected. Like so many of his decisions, Turner's Cabinet represented a kind of half-way house, the product of conflicting pressures that preyed upon a surprisingly indecisive leader. The structure was clearly different, in keeping with Turner's objections to the size and functioning of Trudeau's Cabinets. The number of ministers was reduced from 36 to 29, partly by eliminating the ministries of state for economic development and social development, partly by heaping two and even three portfolios upon individual ministers, an unsustainable burden even Turner himself conceded in calling his changes "Phase One" of Cabinet reform. The change in structure, however, was not matched by a change in personnel. Five new ministers were chosen, but none of them were made members of the Priorities and Planning Committee, in effect the inner Cabinet. Chretien became Minister of External Affairs, a portfolio commensurate with his prestige and popularity, but this masked the bitter in-fighting between the two men in the interregnum between the convention and the selection of the Cabinet. Chretien had emerged hurt and angry from that convention, apportioning a fair measure of blame for his defeat to Quebec ministers such as Ouellet and Lalonde who had supported Turner. He demanded that Turner turn over to him control of Liberal Party affairs in Quebec, including patronage and organization. Turner obviously could not agree, since he had delegated responsibility for Quebec to Ouellet in the leadership campaign, and Ouellet, aided by Quebec's premier Liberal organizer, Jean-Claude Dansereau, had blunted Chretien's efforts to sweep Quebec as a favorite son. Caught between Chretien's angry sense of betrayal and his own debt to Ouellet, Turner could devise only a troika of three ministers to control the Quebec organization — Chretien, Ouellet and Lalonde. The troika was a sham, and everybody in Quebec knew it. Indeed, the in-fighting among the three continued throughout the election campaign.

Lalonde's re-appointment as Minister of Finance dumbfounded Turner's advisers, including Lee, who had been his leadership campaign director. Lalonde epitomized the public's perception of the previous Liberal regime. True, Lalonde had worked quietly for Turner behind-the-scene during the leadership campaign and had agreed to don a Turner button had a third ballot been necessary, but by re-appointing him the new Prime Minister sent the clearest possible signal to the country that he might not after all be the candidate of change. Not only did Turner re-appoint Lalonde, but he also heeded his advice in forming the Cabinet. Turner's advisers — and some English-speaking senior ministers — urged him to reach into the Quebec caucus for backbenchers such as Remi Bujold, Dennis Dawson, Pierre Deniger and Jean Lapierre to give the party a new look in Quebec after Trudeau's departure and the unexpected decision of Health Minister Monique Begin to leave politics. Lalonde, however, objected to the nominations of these young Turks, confident that the Liberals could hold most of their Quebec fortress. Only Lapierre, 28, was appointed, earning the distinction of being Canada's youngest and shortest-lived Cabinet minister.

The Cabinet appointments dampened expectations of change; the patronage appointments of Liberal MPs drowned them. Patronage has always been, for better or worse, part of the fabric of Canadian politics, and politicians of every party assumed a wide degree of public indifference to the issue. That indeed was the prevailing belief among Liberal ministers and MPs when rumors began circulating in the capital about a farewell shower of favors for retiring Liberal MPs and Trudeau staff members. Few, however, anticipated the scope of the farewell — 19 former Liberal ministers, and MPs and organizers received appointments, the most egregious being that of MP Bryce Mackasey as Ambassador to Portugal. Trudeau presented his successor with his staggering list at a meeting in the week before the change of governments. Turner was apparently appalled, and told an aide after the meeting, "turn away when I tell you this because you're going to vomit." Trudeau volunteered to make the appointments before he left office, a course of action his principal secretary, Tom Axworthy, recommended to Turner so that whatever political opprobrium might attend the appointments would stick to Trudeau . Turner, however, demurred. He had nominees of his own for the list, including former Trudeau ministers he did not wish to include in his own Cabinet. He also insisted later that he had received advice from Privy Council Clerk Gordon Osbaldeston to the effect that the appointments, by depriving the Liberals of their majority in the Commons, might persuade Governor-General Jeanne Sauvé to resist a request for dissolution and an election. Circumventing that potential constitutional difficulty required Turner to announce the appointments only after securing the dissolution. So deep was the mutual distrust between the two men that Trudeau insisted that his successor sign a letter committing himself to making the appointments. This letter — and the constitutional advice — were the genesis of Turner's later argument that "I had no option". The distinguished constitutional expert, Eugene Forsey, dismissed the argument as "rubbish". Other constitutional experts agreed in slightly less pithy language. Indeed, Turner soon found himself alone with his argument of constitutional necessity. Ranged against him were constitutional experts, the opposition parties and as it turned out, the voters. Indeed, the Liberals were shocked by the howl of protest from across the country at the appointments which were seen as the ultimate flick of arrogance from a party too long in power. Worse still, Turner had seriously eroded at a single stroke his two major advantages — that he represented change, and that he would be a strong leader.

Shortly after the campaign began, the television networks proposed debates among the party leaders. Turner did not favor a debate, whereas the Conservatives immediately demanded a series of them, and the NDP wanted whatever kind of debate it could get. Turner's advisers, however, believed the political risk in refusing to debate outweighed that of losing a narrow decision to Mulroney. But to minimize the impact of the debate, and to give Turner time to make up for a poor performance, the Liberals insisted that only two debates be held, one in French and one in English. They won their point after protracted negotiations: the debates were set for July 24 and 25. The French debate delivered a body blow to the Liberal campaign; the English debate a jolt to the head. In Quebec, the number of voters without an identification with any federal party climbed from 8 per cent to 33 per cent in the days following the debate, and the percentage of undecided voters soared. Both developments spelled bad news for the Liberal majority party in Quebec. Turner, an intense, nervous person in public at the best of times, never looked comfortable in the French debate against a native Quebecker vastly more at ease in the French language and idiom. The next day, the French press unanimously declared Mulroney the winner. The Tories' bandwagon in Quebec began rolling, finding in its way the image but not the substance of a well-organized adversary. In riding after riding — and for the first time since 1958 — the Conservatives had more money, volunteers, enthusiasm, and organization than the Liberals.

The English debate brought equally doleful results for the Liberals. Turner's briefings for the debate were demonstrably inadequate since he made several factual errors, including the claim that Manitoba had experienced a net loss of population. (He later apologized to the Premier and people of Manitoba.) His nervousness was again cruelly exposed by the merciless eye of the television camera. And once again, he was pushed and pulled by conflicting advice. In the minutes before the debate, Keith Davey was trying to persuade the Prime Minister to attack Mulroney and sound like a reformer, while Bill Lee was urging him to appear statesmanlike and to put distance between himself and the Trudeau regime. Turner had been advised before the debates to play down the patronage issue. But to the consternation and amazement of his advisers, he re-opened the issue late in the English debate, and got clobbered. Trying to score a point on Mulroney for having promised Tories all manner of patronage appointments, Turner found himself put immediately on the defensive, and he repeated his familiar "I had no option" defence. Mulroney replied with lines the television networks subsequently chose for the highlight of the debate: "You had an option. You could have said this was wrong. Instead, you said yes to the old system and the old attitudes. You could have done better." The Turner campaign, by then staggering, was effectively over although Turner kept on campaigning the way a dead man's fingernails continue to grow.

Turner did not seem to be able to avoid embarrassment. In a jocular moment, he patted party president Iona Campagnolo's rear end (to her everlasting credit, she returned the gesture). CTV captured the incident on film but considered it incidental. When Turner repeated the gesture, this time to Lise St. Martin-Tremblay, CTV reckoned it had a story. Instead of apologizing immediately, Turner laughed off the whole affair, an indifference that compounded the damage. Only during the women's debate in August did Turner offer an apology to those who found such behavior inappropriate in the 1980s. The apology did not ease the sting of NDP leader Ed Broadbent's putdown during the French language debate: "What can I say...I think it's a question of generations."

Turner's campaign tour continued to experience organizational hitches, the media turned almost universally hostile, the mid-campaign polls predicted a disastrous result, and panic exacerbated the bitter in-fighting among Turner's advisers. Although Turner had secured the support of many prominent Cabinet ministers for his leadership campaign, his personal advisers and friends were largely drawn from outside the political arena of the Trudeau years. This applied to campaign director Lee, principal secretary John Swift, executive assistant Michael Hunter, general adviser Payne, and others. They too shared a profound skepticism of the Trudeau legacy. But the inevitable result was a lack of hands-on political experience in the previous 16 years. Their skepticism also divorced them from the prominent holdovers in the Liberal Party who wished to defend, if not cherish, the Trudeau legacy. Thus began the ferocious internecine struggle for the mind of Turner and for the direction of the Liberal Party under his leadership, and it grew in direct proportion to the party's decline in the polls. This split in the Turner circle of advisers blew wide open in mid-campaign. With the Liberals' own polls predicting disaster, communications all but broke down between the Prime Minister's Office under Swift and the campaign office under Lee. Ministers such as Lalonde, Erola and Herb Gray, all members of the campaign committee, demanded that Lee be replaced by Keith Davey. Pollsters Reid and Goldfarb were offering conflicting advice. Senator Jerry Grafstein, a Trudeau holdover who had always been close to Turner, wrote an early memorandum about the campaign which was reported to *Maclean's*. Grafstein complained about his leader's handling of the language issue, about being a "flame-thrower" for provincial rights, and about Turner's emphasis on balancing the budget. "(You) are sending out a signal to the Trudeau coalition — the emerging middle class, youth, women and minorities — that thems that have are going to keep it," wrote Grafstein, "and thems that don't have it are going to find it hard to get." Grafstein continued with a prophetic warning: "If you continue to take a course veering to the right, you will pay for it if there is a downward trend in the polls...Of more importance to us both, the Liberal Party will pay a price if we allow our support to erode, particularly in Quebec. Quebec has stood with the Liberal Party because we stood by Quebec. By moving to the right, you allow Mulroney to step into Trudeau's shoes, gaining in Quebec and Ontario and losing marginally in the East and West. Mulroney is moving in Quebec and with the minorities. Both must be stopped." Grafstein, too, found himself on the receiving end of criticism. Lee charged that he had demanded, but never received, a detailed accounting from Red Leaf Communications, the umbrella group of Liberal advertising experts directed by Grafstein. Similarly, the two men fought over Lee's contention that the negative television advertising planned by Grafstein was inappropriate.

With these policy and personality conflicts raging around Turner, Lee decided to bring matters to a head. He wrote his boss a stiff three-page memorandum deploring the state of the campaign and warning that the Liberals were heading towards a crushing defeat. Lee demanded fresh instructions from Turner, giving him as campaign director complete authority over the management of the campaign. Instead, Turner removed Lee from his job and bowed to internal party pressure to bring back Davey, the very man who symbolized much that Turner had promised to change in the Liberal party. Davey immediately persuaded Turner to accept some of his tried and true campaign methods. Reporters' access to the Prime Minister was severely limited. Speeches on deficit reduction gave way to an emphasis on social policy. Promises were made almost daily, the most important being a youth training program. Turner's speeches increasingly featured sharp attacks on Mulroney, complemented by television advertisements slashing away at the cost of Conservative promises and the closing of the Iron Ore Co. of Canada's operation at Schefferville during Mulroney's tenure as company president. Having destroyed his own credibility with a series of gaffes, Turner set about trying to tear down his opponent's. But the Conservatives' lead could not be reduced; in fact, it widened, especially in Quebec where the Tory landslide gathered momentum in the final stages of the campaign.

Quebec Liberals, accustomed to elections without vigorous and well-organized opposition, were completely unprepared for the massive public switch to the Conservatives. Turner had made little personal impact in the province during the leadership campaign; if anything, he finished in a weaker position than he had begun. The much-publicized Liberal machine turned out to be a myth. André Ouellet, a Liberal shogun, could not find even sufficient volunteers to distribute his pamphlet which depicted, in a way that revealed volumes about the way the Liberals had played politics in Quebec, the federally funded projects he had secured for his riding, and listed total federal spending for his constituents, including old age pensions and family allowances. Desperate negotiations began to bring Trudeau to the party's rescue in Quebec. No greater humiliation could have been designed for his successor who gathered up the remnants of his tattered pride and refused to sanction a rally attended by Trudeau and himself. The former prime minister, of course, resisted pressure to assist the successor he so disliked, but he eventually relented in the face of insistent demands from Lalonde and Davey. He attended a rally on the Friday night before election day in the church basement in the east end of Montreal where four months before only 50 Liberals had congregated for a delegate-selection meeting. He spoke briefly, mentioning Turner only once. His was a loon's call before the terrible storm.

The very magnitude of the Liberal defeat saved Turner's political future. He trailed in Vancouver Quadra until the last few days of the campaign when many voters there, appreciating that they would see the Liberals defeated across the country, felt free to cast their ballots for a party leader who had staked his future on their support. Turner won Vancouver Quadra by 3,324 votes.

Seldom in Canadian political history have so many hopes been blasted as quickly as they were by Turner's performance as Liberal leader and Prime Minister. What had seemed pre-ordained to him and to so many in his party, turned out to be an illusion.

THE BUTTERY-SMOOTH CONSERVATIVES

by Val Sears

Mr. Sears is Political Editor of the Toronto Star, based in Ottawa. He is one of the best known and most experienced political reporters in Canada.

When Prime Minister Turner walked into the National Press Theatre in Ottawa and told a hundred frantically scribbling journalists that there would be a national election on September 4, no one was more surprised than the leader of the Progressive Conservative party, Brian Mulroney. "I was the last holdout in our group on the day," he would say later. "I kept saying he wouldn't go until fall. He knew we were ready and he wasn't. I couldn't believe it when he made the announcement."

Mulroney and his team were indeed ready for an election, while the Liberals were going into election worse prepared than Ethelred the Unready.

There was, first of all, the question of money, the mother's milk of politics. The Tories, thanks largely to a slick, mail campaign in 1983, had raised $14,108,012, almost twice as much as the Liberals. While, under the Election Act, no party could spend more than $6.4 million on the actual campaign, the Tory run-up was well-oiled. And Mulroney had what turned out to be a priceless asset — Ontario's Big Blue Machine, and particularly its chief mechanic, Norman Atkins.

Atkins, at 50, was the Godfather of Ontario politics, a gentle man who looks as though he came from Chicago's south side with something lethal in his violin case. He owns an advertising and public relations firm. He had run four campaigns for Premier William Davis of Ontario, and spun off a couple for Richard Hatfield of New Brunswick and Brian Peckford in Newfoundland. Atkins brought with him Pat Kinsella who had started off as an advance man for the Ontario Tories and most recently had run an impeccable campaign for Bill Bennett in British Columbia. Together they were to run a campaign for Mulroney that was buttery smooth if a trifle short on beef.

There had been some uneasiness in the Mulroney organization, which was largely based on his Quebec college-days friends, about turning the campaign over to the Ontario machine. But Mulroney insisted. He felt then that the election would be won or lost in Ontario, and Atkins would enlist Davis, the premier, and all his clout on the side of the federal Conservatives.

Then there was the vital matter of Mulroney's own readiness. During the three months of the Liberal leadership campaign — while media attention had been focussed on that bloodless contest — Mulroney had been at work on test runs in the boonies. He had trotted back and forth across the country — 25,000 miles in all, trying out his speech in various forms in church basements and school auditoriums. He and Atkins had worked on his strengths, repaired his weaknesses. He and his perky wife, Mila, had shaken a thousand hands. They were already into the rhythm of a campaign.

They even had the beginnings of a policy. In Prince Albert, during that spring foray, Mulroney had laid out a five-point package of policy that, he said, would produce "tens upon tens of thousands of new jobs", a statement that would come back to haunt him after his election victory. The centrepiece of the package was a statement on energy in which he promised that the Liberal government's Petroleum and Gas Revenue Tax, a levy on gross revenues of oil firms, would be replaced by a tax on gross profits. There would also be changes in the Petroleum Incentives Program (PIP) under which Ottawa dispensed an estimated $1.6 billion in grants to Canadian oil companies for exploration in the Arctic and East Coast. He would eliminate the "back-in" provision which gave publicly-owned Petro-Canada the right to obtain a retroactive 25 percent ownership of any new oil fields found in lands under federal jurisdiction.

He promised, as well, to lift the 9 percent federal sales tax on fuel for farm machinery, and the capital gains tax on any farms sold to people keeping them in production. These programs, aimed at the West, were estimated to cost from $5 to $6 billion in a study prepared for finance critic John Crosbie who let the figures slip out in a document that reporters sneaked a peek at. The Crosbie paper also said that the total policy package would cost more than $20 billion. He was later told by Mulroney to keep his mouth shut during the rest of the campaign.

Mulroney was happier simply to say: "We are inheriting the biggest mother of a mess ever inflicted on anyone." And as he returned from the Western trip to hear that the Prime Minister had named the election date, he announced: "Hang on to your hat. It's going to be a campaign like you haven't seen in 25 years".

The first issue that had Mulroney waving his own hat — a bonus that would effect the whole campaign — was patronage. In the dying days of his administration Prime Minister Pierre Trudeau decided to reward a long list of MPs and others with patronage appointments. Mulroney was ecstatic. Here was the very issue to expose old-style Grit politics. His policy advisor, Charles MacMillan — described in the Tory office as the party's "token intellectual" — quickly estimated the cost of the appointments at $84 million, "the equivalent," as Mulroney gleefully told audiences, "of a $70 Christmas bonus for senior citizens on the Guaranteed Income Supplement." The Tory leader was off and running around the first lap, while Turner squirmed and said he had no option but to make the Trudeau appointments. "The devil made him do it," laughed Mulroney and the partisan audiences jeered and applauded.

Then Mulroney got hit by a brick on the very issue he was peddling so successfully. On July 14, on a plane trip from the North Shore of Quebec to Montreal, Mulroney came back to chat with reporters. Asked why he was so vehement in his attacks on Liberal patronage when he had promised government jobs for Tories, Mulroney replies: "I was talking to Tories then, and that's what they want to hear. Talking to the Canadian public during an election campaign is something else." Of the appointment of Liberal Bryce Mackasey, he said: "There is no whore like an old whore. If I had been in Bryce's position, I'd have been in there with my nose in the public trough like the rest of them."

In a casual aside, Mulroney said to reporters that his remarks, of course, were off the record. But one journalist, Neil MacDonald of the Ottawa Citizen, would not accept that such a caution, after the remarks were made, was valid. He quoted Mulroney extensively in his newspaper. The effect on the Mulroney people was devastating. Here was their white-hatted hero in the same trough as the villains. It appeared a prime issue was to be lost. Then, battered by advice from both sides about whether to ignore the issue or face it, Mulroney made his decision: he would apologise. In Sault Ste. Marie, four days later, white-faced and nervous, with Mila by his side, Mulroney said he was sorry he had "joked" about the issue of patronage, that he had not meant the remarks to be taken seriously, and that he "very much regretted" treating the matter in the way he had. He would, he said, overhaul the entire patronage system after he was elected. It was the right decision to make and it took the heat off. Mulroney could return to Liberal patronage ... and he did. Later, the Tory leader was to tell a reporter, the apology was a vital political difference — a matter of instinct — between himself and Turner. "I apologised for what I said about patronage. I knew I had to do it. But I never really appreciated how important it was until Turner did not (apologise for patting female bottoms.)"

Mulroney was also now beginning to get his speeches into a dependable format, blurring details but emphasizing the generalities that were to serve him through the rest of the campaign. The basis of his pitch was simple: jokes, Liberal-bashing, NDP-kicking — and a healthy dose of patriotism. There was also the vital and recurring theme of change. One typical speech early in the campaign, given to a rally in Toronto, began this way: "Over the next fifty days, the Progressive Conservative party will be offering Canadians a strong and responsible alternative to the Liberals status quo. We will be offering new people, new ideas and a new approach to government. We will be offering change. Change from the attitudes which have led to confrontation and division between Ottawa and the provinces. Change from the fiscal irresponsibility of successive Liberal governments and the disastrous budgets of four recent finance ministers, John Turner, Allan J. MacEachen, Jean Chretien and now Marc Lalonde. Change from the Liberal certainty of rising interest rates and a falling dollar."

That theme — change — was to be the leitmotif of the entire race ... on both sides. Turner knew he had to be an agent of change from the Trudeau days. Mulroney knew he had to stick Turner with the Liberalism of patronage, staleness, general public bad temper and (relatively) bad times.

One of the distinctions Mulroney offered was a different attitude toward Quebec, rather than refighting, as Turner did, the old separatist issue. In Sept Iles, in early August, Mulroney said the Liberals had turned Canada into a sort of "combat area within which the provinces are in constant conflict. The role of the federal government is that of a Machiavellian policeman whose role is to maintain a semblance of equilibrium by pitting the provinces one against the other. Those who view Canadian federalism as a power struggle naturally seek to usurp provincial jurisdiction. That was the Liberals' favorite sport. Nothing could be more contrary to the spirit of our constitution and nothing more surely provoke provincial distrust. In the performance of its federal responsibilities, a Progressive Conservative government will be guided by the principle of respect for provincial authority."

Mulroney also made clear he was ready to work with anyone in the province — even the Parti Quebecois — to bring about this new era of co-operation. The Pequistes were ready to help. On August 15, Quebec cultural affairs minister Clement Richard said Parti Quebecois members want "anyone but Liberals" to win the election. "It couldn't possibly be worse with the Progressive Conservatives," he said. "Lots of my colleagues feel that way and I'm sure a lot of other people do too." It seemed that the Liberals' stranglehold on Quebec was weakening. The guessing at mid-campaign was for perhaps five or six Tory seats in that province.

In Ontario, the key province, Mulroney talked of social justice. "Our action plan is straightforward," he told a Kitchener audience: "First, we will extend the spousal allowance to eligible widows and widowers between the ages of 60 and 65, regardless of the age of their spouses at death. Second, we will restore at the earliest moment full indexing of the old age pension to the actual cost of living on a quarterly basis. Third, we will increase the guaranteed income supplement as soon as resources permit."

Out on the prairies he talked of new, changed, agricultural and energy policies; in British Columbia, of a new deal for forestry and resources. And there was some wit and humor. One line, repeated over and over, was about how worried he was when the doctor told him he was "sound as a dollar." The rhetorical windup: "We're building one Canada, strong and powerful, fair and united, built on tolerance and opportunity and that's what the election is all about. It's about change, about new beginnings. It's about a period of reconciliation...new prosperity... new unity...a new day for Canada." The audiences, mostly partisan, loved it and applauded wildly, shaking Mulroney's hand afterwards, embracing a smiling Mila.

In July, Turner had made a crucial decision. He would run in British Columbia, in Vancouver Quadra, a mostly upper-income riding that included the University of British Columbia which he had attended. Mulroney was torn. Should he stay in Central Nova in Nova Scotia which he could win easily and which would free him to campaign around the country? Or should he try in Quebec, the relatively safe riding of Brome-Mississqua perhaps, a constituency that had gone Tory before? But in the end, perhaps inevitably, he chose Manicouagan, the riding on the north shore of the St. Lawrence which includes Baie Comeau, the town where he was born, a small town where he had "dreamed big dreams". But it was a gamble. Or so it seemed. The sitting member, a Liberal of course, was Andre Maltais, a popular man who had a majority of 16,655 in 1980. Mulroney's campaign was a model of simplicity. His number one theme was that, as prime minister, he would bring prosperity to the North Shore. He had to add, defensively, that while, as president of Iron Ore Company of Canada, he had had to close the mining town of Schefferville, nearby, the decision was really made in the Cleveland head office. He had had no option. Hanna Mining, the parent company, made him do it. He would not attack Maltais who had worked hard for the riding. But he did lean heavily on the strong, local, nationalist tradition. Wherever he went, speaking in the riding, he was introduced as "the next Prime Minister of Canada." Support was building up from the unions, the local mayors and the riding's Indians. As the Anglican archdeacon, Rev. Bob Bryan, said in mid-August: "There's been growing discontent along the North Shore, including among the fishermen who feel the federal government is content to have them go on welfare. Most of the people I talk to think a change might help." Mulroney was ready to offer it.

Mulroney was anxious to debate Turner on television. The lesson from previous television encounters, both in Canada and the United States, was that "the winner" would be the man who exceeded public expectations in his performance. So Mulroney challenged Turner, at a news conference on July 9, and Turner reluctantly agreed. Turner's hope was to appear managerial, competent, in charge, a new man, with a new approach. But Mulroney had advantages: he spoke French with a local casualness that was better than Turner's, and expectations of him were not so high. The French debate centered on the economy. Turner called Mulroney "the $20 billion man" for apparently being prepared to increase the federal deficit by that amount to stimulate the economy. Mulroney, fighting back, said Turner, a former Minister of Finance, was "the father of deficits in Canada." Mulroney, looking relaxed and confident, reminded the audience that many of the problems they were discussing were the result of "nearly 21 years of uninterrupted Liberal rule." Turner, nervous, occasionally grasping for the right French words, scored fewer points. The next day, the Quebec newspapers gave Mulroney Round One. "First match: advantage to Mulroney", was the headline in Le Journal de Montreal, the province's largest circulation newspaper. "Mulroney emerges the winner in the first debate of the chiefs," was the headline in Montreal's La Presse. Le Devoir said Turner appeared to be on the defensive. The English-language Gazette of Montreal also gave the debate to Mulroney. Decima Research, the Tory's polling organization, told Mulroney the impact was "historically startling." Mulroney was jubilant. He had, as biographer L. Ian MacDonald wrote, "begun to establish himself in the minds of Quebec voters as a favorite son and prospective prime minister."

But the second, English, debate was the real Mulroney triumph. As in most such encounters, the impact was not immediate. The newspapers had to digest the result, and much of the triumph was by word of mouth. But there seemed little question, even in the moments after, that Mulroney was more aggressive and knew how to milk the cameras. Turner was again nervous, licking his lips, appearing defensive. The newspapers the next day were unanimous: Mulroney had won. The Winnipeg Sun said Mulroney triumphed "hands down"; Turner was "bloodied" said the Vancouver Sun; in the Atlantic provinces, journalists and publishers declared Mulroney the winner. The high-point in the debate for Mulroney came within 20 minutes of the end of the two-hour ordeal. It will likely live in both men's memory forever.

Turner inexplicably brought up the patronage issue, taunting Mulroney: "I have been saying the same thing to my party on all the issues that I say to the country. We have this patronage issue brought up earlier. Mr. Mulroney has not been dealing with the issue in the same way. He told his party last year that every available job would be made available to every living, breathing Conservative."

"I beg your pardon, sir," Mulroney replied.

"I would say, Mr. Mulroney," Turner went on, "that on the basis of what you've talked about — getting your nose in the public trough — that you wouldn't offer any newness in the style of government."

Mulroney was ready. Jaw thrust out, wrapped in righteousness, he struck.

"The only person who has ever appointed anyone around here for the last 20 years has been your party; and 99 percent have been Liberals, and you ought not to be proud of that. I have apologized to the Canadian people for kidding about it. The least you should do is apologize for having made these horrible appointments."

"Well," Turner replied, "I have told you and told the Canadian people, Mr. Mulroney, that I had no option."

"You had an option, sir," Mulroney shot back. "You could have said: 'I'm not going to do it.' This is wrong for Canada. And I am not going to ask Canadians to pay the price. You had an option, sir, to say no, and you chose to say yes, yes to the old attitudes, and the old stories of the Liberal party."

Weakly, Turner replied, "I had no option. I..."

Mulroney was relentless: "That was an avowal of failure. That is a confession of non-leadership, and this country needs leadership. You had an option, sir, you could have done better."

The two-minute exchange was devastating. Mulroney was to live it over and over again, in private and on the platform. "I hit him once," he told an interviewer later, smacking his fist into his palm. "I hit him again, pow." Another smack. "He went down. You know, (Ontario premier) Bill Davis called me the next morning and said it was the most dramatic six seconds on television he had ever seen."

Certainly, it was effective on the campaign, even for those who did not watch the debates. Time and time again, Mulroney would thunder: "Turner could have said no." Or he would sneer: "The devil made him do it. He had no option." The audiences roared.

Clearly, the debates changed things. The CROP poll in The Globe and Mail showed 44 percent of the respondents watched the English debate, and 47 percent judged Mulroney the winner. "People were in the mood to kick ass," Mulroney's press secretary Bill Fox told biographer MacDonald.

The women's issue debate, three weeks later, was less decisive. Mulroney did not do as well. Throughout the campaign, there was a perception, reported but never really documented, that Mulroney did not score well with women. There was a sense that he was a chauvinist on women's issues, too glib, and too much of the locker-room jock about him, too much of the travelling salesman and the farmer's daughter. Because of the format of the debate, Mulroney was not asked about his stand on abortion and his responses to other questions of particular interest to women were generalized and tentative. Turner accused Conservatives of being opposed to social programs that mainly involved women and Mulroney replied that he was "earnestly and genuinely committed" to correcting past injustices to women in employment and social benefits.

But by mid-August it probably did not matter. A poll conducted for Southam News indicated the Conservatives had a healthy lead over the Liberals. About 51 percent of the voters polled said they would back the Tories, compared to 32 percent for the Liberals.

And while Turner was making mistakes, Mulroney's campaign, managed by Atkins and Kinsella, was gliding along its buttery way. Seldom had there been a tour more carefully and successfully arranged. Mulroney's aircraft, chartered from Air Canada and dubbed Manicouagan I, wafted him from one end of the country to the other, accompanied by a raddled press corps, whirring cameras and blinding lights.

On the ground, Mulroney's tour bus was a combination office and daytime home. In the back was a compartment with nubbly brown walls, telephone, television set and sofa, where Mulroney and Mila could retire between appearances to refresh themselves with Perrier and doughnuts. Aboard the plane was a tonne of equipment, plus 36 support staff. Before appearing at the door of the bus or aircraft, Mulroney had read a briefing book on the riding to be visited, a biography of the candidate, along with do's and don'ts about personal questions. There was a detailed map showing the route into the auditorium in which he would speak and an inch-thick packet of photocopied clippings from yesterday's newspapers about the campaign.

His strategy by mid-August was clear: Make a few policy speeches then shut up and coast. His policy positions were now well rehearsed, with only the cost still at issue. Here is where Mulroney stood on some of the central issues of the campaign:

Unemployment — Mulroney would create a $250 million program of tax credits for businesses which made jobs for young people. He would also convene a federal-provincial conference to study all aspects of youth employment. Grants up to $25,000 to help young people create their own jobs would be considered.

Abortion — Supported the existing law which says abortion is legal only when performed in accredited hospitals with the approval of a committee of doctors who determine the woman's health is endangered by the pregnancy.

Nuclear arms freeze — Support for a nuclear arms freeze that is verifiable on condition that it would not give one side superiority over the other.

Capital punishment — Personally opposed but would support a free vote in parliament.

Taxation — Would devise a fairer and simpler tax system and force wealthy Canadians to pay a "handsome" minimum tax.

Patronage — Would set up a parliamentary committee to review patronage appointments. (But he would not make clear which appointments would be reviewed.)

Free trade with the U.S. — Would "pursue bilateral discussions with the United States on specific sectors."

Regularly attacked by Turner with the charge that the Tories would cut medicare, Mulroney was forced to defend it over and over again, finally calling it a "sacred trust". "A Progressive Conservative government will vigorously defend the integrity of universal health care," he said. "Our medicare system was started in 1957 with the passage of universal hospital insurance by the Conservative government of the day. It was the government of John Diefenbaker and the Hall Royal Commisssion on Health Care which provided the basic framework for medicare. The Progressive Conservative party has defended medicare ever since. We believe we have an obligation to strengthen medicare through adequate funding and, where possible, to improve it."

His main thrust throughout was jobs, jobs, jobs. It would be up to the private sector to provide them, but a Tory government would set the framework with, among other things, lower interest rates. "A Progressive Conservative government," Mulroney said, "will give Canadians lower interest rates through a higher dollar. We will strengthen the dollar by renewing investor confidence in Canada — the kind of confidence investors always had in our country until these 20 years of Liberal government wiped it out. We will win back for Canada its reputation as a country that welcomes initiatives and entrepreneurship...as a nation that offers a hand to help, but keeps its fingers out of your businesses and your lives."

While foreign policy did not loom large in Mulroney's campaign speeches he made clear he would welcome and work for a closer relationship with the United States, emphasized his friendship with President Ronald Reagan, and said that when anything was an issue between the United States and the world, he would give Washington "the benefit of the doubt." He also promised to increase spending on Canada's defence establishment and restore the distinctive uniforms to the armed forces.

All of these promises made costs an issue in the campaign, with Turner insisting that Mulroney reveal how much his promises were worth and Mulroney saying that all would be revealed in due time. But it was not until almost the end of the campaign, in an address to the Empire and Canadian Clubs of Toronto on August 28, that Mulroney took up the challenge and put his own price on his promises. "Our estimate is that the gross incremental cost in Year One of our proposed strategy — the revenue foregone and new investment — will be approximately $1.7 billion or about one and a half percent of current government spending. Our plans for Year Two — fiscal 1986-87 — have a gross cost of $2.1 billion in cost outlays. Our fiscal framework calls for little, if any, overall increase in discretionary spending, as we plan to finance these investments through a reduction in government overhead expenses, program reallocations and tax reform. We are confident that by spending smarter — by investing in more productive purposes, by enhancing productivity, by increasing the competitiveness of key export industries, by engendering genuine federal-provincial cooperation, by civilizing our labor unions, and by prudent management of government finances, we can stimulate the growth and create the jobs which will start the deficit on a downward course."

It was a large order and Turner scoffed. He estimated the cost of Tory promises at closer to $20 billion. But by now the campaign was so far along, that the costs meant nothing and few Canadians could absorb numbers of that order, much less make any political decision on them. Everywhere, in Quebec, Ontario and the West, judging both from the polls and the reports of travelling media,

Mulroney was pulling far ahead. There was every indication of a sweep. The big breakthrough had come in Quebec, the base from which Liberal electoral power sprang. The Tories had won a majority there only once in this century, the Diefenbaker win in 1958. But now the base was crumbling under the able guidance of Mulroney's Quebec chairman, Bernard Roy. "I'm telling you," Roy said in mid-August, "there's a complete turnaround. The Liberals are coming apart at the seams. We could go as high as 50 or 60 seats, even some in English Montreal." Mulroney had been campaigning heavily in the province, building on his success in the French debate. He had always known he had a chance to win big there. He spoke idiomatic French, he was a local boy and he had many friends and campaigners in the province. In fact, much of his appeal to delegates at the leadership convention had been the fact he could win seats in French Canada. A Southam poll in early August had shown the Conservatives leading the Liberals in Quebec by a stunning 49 percent to 37 percent. Mulroney's people had put together an organization which called itself Le Tonnere Bleu, Blue Thunder, and they had been busy recruiting local candidates on the oldest political theme in the world — "It's time for a change." Crowds were building up for Mulroney rallies, 1,000 at a corn roast in the South Shore riding of Vercheres, more than 1,000 in downtown Montreal. And Premier Rene Levesque was helping as well, not only by declaring his admiration for Mulroney's flexibility in federal-provincial relations but by putting the boots to the separatist Parti Nationaliste (PN), a spinoff from the PQ which hoped to capture some federal seats. The Quebec premier regularly belittled the "separatist federalists" and cleared the way for two-way Tory-Liberal confrontations in most Quebec ridings. Mulroney was prophetic when he told a Sept Iles crowd: "I am convinced that we are witnessing one of those special moments when an entire country turns the page of an era that comes to an end. To restore the health of their democracy," Mulroney claimed, "the men and women of Canada are preparing to throw off the yoke of the Liberal Party, which is now powerless and has nothing more to offer anyone, except its friends. I know that the men and women of Quebec will be part of this renewal. They, more than anyone else, know the cost of putting all their eggs in the Liberal basket. Springtime will arrive early this year. We will have it on September 4."

In Ontario, Atkins had been able to recruit not only the province's Big Blue Machine, the best political organization in the country, but had the enthusiastic endorsement of its leader, Premier Davis. Davis was appearing at rallies around the province, not tepidly as he had for Joe Clark or Robert Stanfield, but with pipe-puffing eagerness. Ontario's vote had always been volatile but Atkins knew that with Quebec still uncertain the Tories had to win at least 50 of Ontario's 95 seats to form a majority government. In 1979, the Tories had won 57 seats in Ontario, but still didn't get a majority because they were virtually wiped out in Quebec. In 1980, the Conservatives dropped to 38 seats in Ontario and were back in opposition. It was clear to the Ontario Conservative chairman, Bill McAleer, that the Liberals would hold on to the ethnic vote — despite Mila's East European appeal — but the rest was soft and the Tories had a "good part of it."

In the West, Liberal hopes — built up in the early days by Turner's Western orientation — were fading fast. Columnist Don Braid said: "The Liberal strategy, such as it was, had two parts: to convince the rubes that voting Liberal is to the West's advantage and to woo New Democratic voters...but the jaws of the pincher have lost their bite." But the heart of the matter was the Tories' almost unassailable base in the West, growing since the days of that prairie populist John Diefenbaker. The West, particularly British Columbia, had felt left out of national decision-making under the Liberals. Now, with a Tory win in sight, they had a chance to get their issues on the agenda again and they leaped at it.

Backing up the television and newspaper coverage of the campaign, was a heavy television ad budget. Mulroney's ads emphasized both his "aw shucks" charm (at first) then, after the debates, his forcefulness and his "prime ministerial image," — at a cost of about $4 million. The Tories saved much of their television ammunition for the final week of the campaign — but it was really only icing on the victory cake.

As election day neared, Mulroney made a final swing through Ontario and headed for Baie Comeau on September 3 to await the result. As always, he put up at the guest house of the old mill manager's home, now Le Manoir de Baie Comeau. On September 4, a misty morning, he and Mila went to the primary school to vote. Then, in the lull of election day, he had time to reflect on the campaign and what he wanted to do with the mandate he was now certain of winning. Earlier, he had told his policy advisor Charlie MacMillan he wanted to be remembered in history for four things: a constitutional settlement with Quebec; restructuring the Canadian economy; achieving a middlepower role for Canada in the world; and an improved economic and social situation for the country's native peoples. As the results began to role in, it was abundantly evident he would get his chance.

The origins of the Mulroney victory, in retrospect, were clear. The principal one was change. Canadians were clearly fed up with the Liberals; the party was stale, old and cynical. It had lost its reputation as a competent manager. It was time to go. Mulroney ran a faultless campaign. Where there were mistakes, they were quickly recognized and corrected. The momentum was right, the organization was impeccable, the money was there and so were the right candidates. Turner's campaign, on the other hand, was a disaster. He seemed not to have an instinct for the political moment. And yet, hindsight suggests nothing would have mattered. Turner and the Liberals were due for the high jump and the voters were happy to oblige.

In Baie Comeau, at one o'clock in the morning, Mulroney made his way to the podium amid such a wave of applause that it was seven minutes after he began "Dear friends..." before he was allowed to speak. "The country has spoken," he finally said, "the real country nurtured by its past sacrifices, by the latent strength of its people, and by its awareness of its place in the world. Canada has responded to a call for unity...to reconciliation and to the definition of new national goals..."

Afterwards, to his friends, Mulroney recalled "one thing I've learned...that's how to keep my eye on the ball. It's going to take me to 24 Sussex Drive."

THE NDP SURVIVORS

by Nick Hills

Mr. Hills, an experienced political reporter, is now General Manager of Southam News, a service providing Canadian and International News to the Southam group of newspapers. He directed the Southam News coverage of the 1984 election.

Shortly before the campaign began, The New Democratic Party's national director, Gerry Caplan, wrote this searing assessment of the Party's problems:

"CONFIDENTIAL
Election 1984: The Strategic Overview.

"It is critical that all our planning for the coming campaign be conceived and executed with an explicit awareness of the advantages and disadvantages for the NDP of the current political situation. We face disturbing problems which, if not minimized, could lead to unhappy electoral consequences..."

A. Disadvantages:

1. We are very low in all the national polls.
2. Everyone knows this.
3. Much of the media has lost interest in us and is writing us off.
4. Some say we are irrelevant to the present moment and there is no purpose in people voting for us.
5. Some say we have nothing new to say, and we are fighting for a better yesterday.
6. Whatever we do or say, some insist it is not new.
7. When we fight to preserve medicare and pensions, or when we emphasize women's issues, we are dismissed for recycling past policies.
8. Both other parties have new leaders, and are treated by some as if new faces are synonymous with new ideas and new directions.
9. We are hurt by the sense that our policies over the years make us the party of big government, big bureaucracy and an outmoded belief in government intervention as a positive tool..."

No impartial observer of the political scene in Canada during the 12 months leading up to the September 4 election would have disagreed with Caplan before the campaign began. The NDP had spent more than two years going through hell. Acrimony and bitterness remained from Ed Broadbent's support of Trudeau's constitutional reforms. Broadbent's own leadership and philosophy had been called into question by such respected figures in the movement as former Saskatchewan premier Allan Blakeney, and the late Grant Notley, leader of the Alberta NDP. One disaffected Saskatchewan member had come within minutes of openly challenging Broadbent for the leadership of the party at the 50th anniversary convention in Regina, July 1, 1983. Above all, the party was in desperate shape in the opinion polls. Between June 1982, and June 1984, the New Democrats had fallen from 23 per cent to 11 per cent in the Gallup Report on Voter Preferences. After the recession took hold, their traditional economic policies became, indeed, unreal, and in the summer months before the election call they were stuck at a level of public support which suggested they would lose more than half of their 30 seats. To make matters worse in the public's perception, the party's own pollster, Larry Ellis, had taken a major sampling of public opinion in British Columbia, Saskatchewan, Manitoba and Ontario, come up with the same sort of results, made his recommendations and then been fired. It looked as though the NDP couldn't face up to the facts, so it shot the messenger. The best that Caplan could say, in the downside part of his internal analysis, was "We can avoid the apocalypse some predict for us, but it is by no means inevitable that we will."

On September 4, less than three months later, the New Democrats not only avoided apocalypse, but were returned to Parliament with more seats in English Canada than the Liberals. Though their popular vote dropped slightly from 19.8 per cent in the 1980 election to just over 19 per cent, its distribution was remarkably fortunate. In Ontario, the political power house of the country, the NDP won 13 seats, up from six at dissolution, and only one less than the Liberals. The campaign had gone so well, at least until the last two weeks, that NDP leaders such as Ontario's Bob Rae and Manitoba premier Howard Pawley had openly predicted the party would become the official opposition. As the vote counting rolled through Thunder Bay on election night, the results in Ontario were so remarkable that even National leader Ed Broadbent took up the cry. But in the West, the Tory tide was simply too massive and the NDP lost seats to end up with a total of 30, just two less than in 1980. It was at least a moral victory clawed from the jaws of defeat, and how it was achieved is a remarkable political story.

The achievement of the New Democrats in basically holding on to what they had won in 1980, in the face of such a gigantic political tide to the Conservatives, can never be underestimated. The internal friction over personalities and policy, prior to the 1983 Regina convention, had put Broadbent in his own particular purgatory. The strains and stresses were such over a prolonged period of time that many other minority or splinter parties would not have survived. When Caplan became national party director in the fall of 1982, the furious debate over what one official called "Broadbents's astonishing decision to commit himself to Trudeau on the spot" on repatriating the constitution, was still going on. He and his leader were faced with a situation where, according to another insider, "lifelong friends did not speak to each other, people actually hated each other-...they would check other people's phone calls. The bitter inter-regional trouble could not be exaggerated, and it undermined Ed's position terribly. This was a massive regional split." For Caplan, trying to right the socialist ship, the whole situation was almost inexplicable. As he admitted later, "I still cannot figure out whether it was a philosophical or a political split."

There had also been trouble at party headquarters. A previous national director, Robin Sears, had been seen as too much the 'leader's man', when he should have been the middle man between leader and party, or even 'the representative' of the party. And Sears' successor, Mary Ellen McQuay, was never happy in her job. A vacuum developed. To make matters even more troubling, James Laxer, the national research director, had embarked on an almost personal campaign to change the political and philosophical bent of

Broadbent himself. He was trying, in particular, to get Broadbent to change his traditional views on deficit financing, to become more of an economic realist. Coming from Laxer, this was extraordinary if not laughable, because he had first made his name in Canadian politics as a leading member of the Waffle group, considered to be ultraradical and left wing. Now Laxer was preaching moderation to his leader. Laxer was warned not to push Broadbent too quickly and too far, but he persisted, even though Broadbent was not really ready for conversion. On October 17, 1982, the CTV network aired a television interview with the NDP leader in which he said "at this point there can be no increase in the federal deficit." Two days later, Broadbent made what was to become a landmark speech. It broke new ground on party policy and caused a new round of dissension among the traditional supporters of the NDP, both inside and outside the leader's circle. In the speech, Broadbent proposed a $2.2 billion job-creation program which would be financed by cuts in other areas of goverment spending, and increased personal taxes on the rich. What is fascinating, in hindsight, is that Broadbent actually advocated cost-cutting programs similar to those introduced by the Conservatives two years later. Aside from a special surtax on high income earners and a 50 per cent reduction in the petroleum incentives program, he proposed that construction of new embassies and residences abroad be slashed; the Canadian Unity Information Office budget be sharply reduced, and the government's information budget be cut by one third. He emphasized that "the special surtax on high income earners and the saving of money through the reduction of present spending would yield the treasury at least $2.2 billion."

As a switch in policy direction, the move seemed modest but it caused no end of trouble for the already embattled leader. It did not seem to matter that the position had been worked out with the national research director. The fallout came thick and fast, particularly from journalist John Ferguson, of Southam News, a serious student of New Democrat policies. On October 17, two days before the Hamilton speech, Ferguson wrote a story for 15 Southam newspapers, which began: "Are Ed Broadbent and the New Democratic Party about to commit political suicide? On Tuesday, Broadbent will tell a Hamilton meeting of the Canadian Club that the NDP has replaced its longstanding call for an income tax cut to pull the economy out of a slump, with a new-found concern about the $20-million-plus deficit. Insiders say Broadbent will deliver a major policy speech adopting the basic Liberal party line that spending should be cut in some programs — not social programs — to free up money for job creation." Ferguson's interpretation of this change was politically damning: "The NDP has been alone in calling for a tax cut. Shelving that demand will leave the party on the same turf as the Conservatives and, even worse politically, the same as the Liberals." He went on to report that the NDP's sudden concern about the deficit apparently was based on polls showing people doubted the NDP's ability to govern the country in such economic times, and was designed to broaden the party's base on the right. He suggested the switch might go down as the biggest political blunder since Joe Clark's flip-flop over the same question when he became Prime Minister in 1979. Within the NDP itself, Ferguson said, it might be nearly as divisive as Broadbent's hasty support of Trudeau's constitutional proposals in the fall of 1980.

Two weeks later, the same journalist dispatched another report to Southam newspapers suggesting Broadbent might be on a collision course with organized labor and unhappy members of his own caucus. An extraordinary meeting between CLC heavyweights and Broadbent's staff took place. One CLC source commented: "We are not ready to get into a pissing match yet." However, at a party caucus meeting in the last week of October, the leader faced tough questions from some of his colleagues. "In abandoning deficit financing, he's moving away from party policy," said one New Democrat. A labor source added: "What we have with Broadbent's proposal is about half the program that (Liberal Finance Minister) Lalonde gave us last week. It appears we may be on a collision course." The move clearly shifted the NDP away from the official policy of the Canadian Labor Congress with which the New Democrats were meant to be closely allied. More than 2,000 delegates to the CLC biennial convention the previous May in Winnipeg approved detailed economic resolutions which attacked federal and provincial government spending restraints and called for "a personal income tax cut directed to low and moderate income earners to restore lost purchasing power to the lowest income groups."

Yet, whatever the chilling effects within the NDP and organized labor, Broadbent's essentially brave change of economic policy opened up a new debate which in the end proved to be worthwhile. On the one hand, he was attacked by Ontario NDP leader Bob Rae who said, "I have never regarded deficits as the central issue. The central issue is what steps need to be taken to get the economy moving. I think that discussions about deficits are really red herrings." Rae went on, "When I was finance critic at the time of the Clark government, I said that the bottom line of every government's budget has to be people and the bottom line has to be getting the economy moving." On the other hand, the less dogmatic politicians on the Left realized that something had to be done to make NDP policy fit the fears as well as the hopes of all those people who had been so cruelly struck down by the recession. John Fryer, the articulate and ambitious head of the 230,000 member National Union of Provincial Government Employees, commented bitterly, "We are united on platitudes and shibboleths. When it comes to real programs with real answers, we fall short. When we go out knocking on doors and say 'This is our program', people say, 'We don't need more government, look at how they've screwed it up'. What answer do we have to that? None."

Richard Gwyn, the noted political columnist for the Toronto Star, said that Broadbent's Hamilton speech had made history: "Abruptly, NDP leader Ed Broadbent has dragged his party into the centre of the economic debate. His Hamilton speech represents the most dramatic change in party policy since its founding in 1979, and its only real re-thinking of policy since Broadbent, then a back-bencher, attempted unsuccessfully in the late '60s to convince his colleagues to accept 'industrial democracy': that is, workers co-managing the companies that employ them, rather than just fighting the managers that employ them...In essence, Broadbent has shifted his party's concern from the redistribution of wealth to the redistribution of the means of producing wealth. He accepts now that all problems can no longer be solved by throwing money at them, and that the size of the deficit may itself be part of the problem." This was a dramatic turnaround, Gwyn argued, because in the current economic debate the NDP had had no part to play: "It has nothing much to say, except that the government should spend more, as if past free spending and the resulting deficits and accumulated national debt were not themselves part of the economic problems that now bedevil us."

The immediate problem for Broadbent, however, was that while he may have shifted his own economic thinking, the party — particularly the caucus — was having a hard time shifting with him. To compound this, it was not clear just how committed Broadbent himself was to the new thinking, and just how strong his resolve was in the face of criticism and even a growing disrespect within party ranks. There were those close to the leader who thought that psychologically and intellectually, he was not, in fact, ready to make the great leap forward. One party official, who saw a lot of Broadbent, said simply, "Ed was not ready to do what Laxer wanted and when the trouble came, Laxer was indifferent to Ed's capacity to deal with such a new direction." On December 16, just two months after his Hamilton speech, Southam News reported that in an interview with two reporters, Broadbent had suggested he no longer opposed an increase in the federal deficit to create jobs and that Finance Minister Lalonde should do just that in his budget expected early in 1983. Broadbent tried to explain that his Hamilton speech meant he had opposed an increase in the deficit only "at this time...the context is crucial. Last fall, it would have been a serious mistake for Lalonde to have simply announced an increase in the deficit without putting in place a serious economic plan for the economy as a whole." He now urged an increase in public sector involvement. There were those inside and outside Broadbent's party who regarded this almost instant change of heart as simply the result of crushing pressure. Certainly, Broadbent gave the impression of being in a tortured state over the issue, and unable to be precise and clear about just exactly where he stood.

Questioner: "You would increase total government spending?"

Broadbent: "Yes, yes. And I want to pursue the analogy and I want it not to be the kind we have with the Liberals and this is absolutely crucial — sort of increase spending because they don't know what's going on in the economy...I want to make sure it goes into productive areas that would create jobs."

Questioner: "So what you are saying now is that you're not overly concerned about the deficit as you said in a couple of interviews (earlier). You said, 'we can't go further into debt.' You said, 'we can't increase the deficit at this time'."

Broadbent: "...it is very important for me to be intellectually honest."

Questioner: "I'm waiting for you to be intellectually honest, Ed."

Broadbent: "...I would argue there's total and absolute consistency because the problem we had last fall grew out of total, colossal mismanagement over a period of time by the Liberals, by Lalonde's predecessor and it bears directly on what one was reading in The New York Times, time after time, and I've never advocated, from an opposition point of view, policies that I thought would be irresponsible..."

The trouble was, of course, that Broadbent was trying to make 'last fall' seem like an age ago. In fact, it was a period of two months. It was difficult to see how the economic situation could have changed so dramatically in such a short period of time to support Broadbent's own change of position on deficit financing. Certainly, an NDP insider, closely involved with party policy and thinking, saw it differently. "The caucus went back for a year to peddling the old bromides it did not really believe in, the orthodox shibboleths about creating jobs."

In the year that followed this debacle, there was no real suggestion that the NDP could come to grips with what ailed it. The opinion polls in 1983 consistently showed the Tories to be at around 50 per cent, with the Liberals trailing badly between the mid-20s and the mid-30s, and the New Democrats holding on to 15 or 16 per cent of the popular vote. At that level of support, and with the Liberals seemingly done for, there were those in the NDP who believed that by some divine right, the Party would climb back to the 20 to 25 per cent level once an election became imminent. On the other hand, there were those like Caplan and Laxer who still believed there had to be some realism injected into policy and strategy if the Party was ever again to rise above the 20-per-cent threshold. And then there were others, mainly in the West, still smarting from the constitutional battles and a feeling that Broadbent, from industrial Oshawa, did not understand or really care about that region of the country which traditionally provided the New Democrats with their main support.

This resulted in two different sets of party principles being produced prior to the 50th anniversary convention in Regina on July 1, 1984. There was a national document and a western document, with the architects of the latter being former Saskatchewan Premier Blakeney, and the highly respected Alberta leader, Notley. On top of this, there was serious talk about a challenge being made to Broadbent's leadership through the usual review procedures of the party. Asked later if he thought there was a sense of frustration at the Regina convention because of the party's failure to make substantial gains in public opinion during the Liberals' sharp slide, Broadbent admitted: "It is true. Without exception, people in the party, from myself as leader to the person who works in the constituency, all hope you are doing better. So there is a sense of frustration when you are not doing better. At the convention people said to themselves, unconsciously or not, well whether or not we have done well as we would have liked, by God we believe in something...The more serious matter for the party convention was the Prairie document that came up for discussion. They (Blakeney and Notley) as provincial leaders ought to have, in my view...brought that document forward within the time limits laid down. But they got working on it late, and they still wanted to have the debate and just sort of throw a monkey wrench into what was to be a celebration, and a well-planned and organized debate...that might have led to a split in the party, but it didn't."

Later party stalwarts, including Broadbent, began to see the Regina convention as the turning point in preparing the party for an election in 1984. In fact, the turning point did not occur until the eve of the election campaign. There were, however, a series of disasters which rammed home to the party that unless it turned sharply away from old orthodoxy involving platform and electoral strategy, the NDP would be annihilated. The first disaster was a report by Laxer attacking Party Policy. The second, third, fourth, and fifth were a series of opinion polls showing the party falling like a stone to around 11 per cent support.

The New Democrats had done their own polling in the fall of 1983 — their first since the 1980 election — and the results were not happy. Pollster Ellis took one look at the numbers and told senior party officials that the NDP was in dire trouble, particularly on the Prairies. The party brass did not dispute the figures; rather, they had little confidence in his personality, convictions and strategy. They had hired him in the first place because there was no one else who could do the surveying in the NDP strongholds for the money available. One of the people responsible says, "He was a Damon Runyon figure from Regina, dark glasses, big boots and a Fu Manchu moustache. We were ambivalent , some doubted his polling techniques, and he was pushy with his preconceptions...but we had no other option." Another added, "We desperately need some data." So what did the results really show, even in the fall of 1983? "That we were slipping," said one official who studied the data. "We still had credibility as the defender of the little guy. But on all issues involving economic management we had very little credibility. This was very personally distressing for Ed (Broadbent) because he had spent so much time in 1979 and 1980 talking about industrial strategy. "The public perception of us had not changed; we were still the same as under David Lewis and Tommy Douglas." Ellis argued, among other things, that the NDP had to persuade people the party was right on economic policies, and that the issue was job, jobs, jobs. "We decided that Ellis was wrong on strategy, not on numbers. He drew the wrong conclusions, but his data saved us. It was credible and we acted on it differently," said the Party official.

While the party was digesting these disturbing polling results, Laxer was preparing his own kind of bomb. He had been research director of the federal party since 1981, and had advised Broadbent that he would be leaving to take up an academic position at York University. He volunteered to write an assessment of NDP economic policy for consideration by the federal caucus prior to the next election. Laxer completed his assessment in January of 1984, as the three parties began preparations for an almost certain election. His report was sent to the NDP caucus — and found its way also to the press. The leak was so deliberate, one could almost say the report was distributed to the press. The result of this mischief was awful for the leader, the caucus and the party. The NDP was in the headlines again, making legitimate news — but it was the wrong kind of news. The report described Party policy as seriously inadequate, contra-dictory, short-sighted and ideologically ambivalent: "The NDP's analysis of economic and social evolution remains locked in the 1950s and 1960s where it had its origins. It is now so seriously out of keeping with the reality of the 1980s that it has become a serious impediment — a barrier to appropriate action rather than a guide to it." Laxer went on to say that "there has been an oddly unsatisfying quality about social democratic pronouncements in Canada in recent years. NDP spokesman have often appeared to be the last defenders of an economic system that is in decline — demanding that it live up to its former greatness. An endless succession of tactical adaptions to the social democratic thought of the past has left the NDP with an economic analysis of little value and an economic program that is a hodge-podge of contradictions and dead-end solutions." In particular, Laxer cited the NDP's longstanding concern to increase economic demand, rather than the problem of economic production.

He scorned the party's focus on unemployment rather than inflation, suggesting that the party was speaking for trade unions whose members could actually protect themselves from inflation through collective bargaining, although such protection was not open to many other Canadian workers. "A political analysis that does not deal with the problem of inflation and a political program which cannot counter its ravages can have limited appeal. The majority of workers who fell behind inflation...could be forgiven for believing the NDP had a 'survival of the fittest' approach to peoples' incomes in which those with strong bargaining power win and others lose." The harshly critical analysis was in the country's newspapers before Broadbent had had time to digest properly what he and his caucus had been handed.

Interestingly, Laxer received some quite positive responses from important people in the NDP. Saskatchewan MP Lorne Nystrom said: "We need to discuss where we're going. Too many of our policies are rooted in the past." Stephen Lewis, the party's highly respected former Ontario leader, said he considered much of Laxer's data to be "compelling." Lewis added that he "wouldn't mind debating some of this. I don't know if he's right or wrong, but if he takes a few cracks at the party, the world doesn't come to an end." However, the establishment view was summed up by the NDP House leader Ian Deans who commented: "We would find it very difficult to put inflation ahead of jobs. We've made that decision. It's a political decision. That doesn't mean we're living in the '30s . Maybe it means we're living in the '80s." National director Caplan, who had just joined party headquarters, was appalled, and could hardly have imagined a worse thing happening at a worse time. Other party officials agreed with him. Said one: "The Laxer report hurt us very, very badly because of his personal reputation. The analysis was taken very, very seriously, and it came at a time when New Democrats were feeling anxious about their economic policies. It hurt us with the media and it hurt us with the general public. "We were making headlines again, but it was about a split — this was another serious blow in our winter of discontent." There were also those who thought that, as an attack on policy, it was unfair. It was a conservative document to many traditional New Democrats, and it argued that the party had no industrial policy. Yet, Broadbent, to his credit, had been talking seriously about industrial strategy for many months. And, ironically, Broadbent and Laxer had seen eye to eye on this issue when Laxer was director of research. It must have seemed like a stab in the back, and one insider said, "Laxer didn't give a damn about the party."

This weeping and wailing may have been excessive, but the party was in real torment over its inability to pick up strength from the staggering Liberals. It didn't need another wound at a time when key members of the party leader's staff and the national director's staff were trying to clear their heads of pessimism and begin hammering out an election campaign strategy that would save the party from electoral disaster. In April and May of 1984, the party had two more public opinion surveys done — but this time by a Vancouver polling company. The party used up all its money, and the surveying took place only in a very limited number of constituencies. Said one official who was privy to the results: "The data showed Gallup was right. We asked questions on the basis we were going to be annihilated, and we got the information we were looking for to plot a survival strategy." In the end, these two surveys produced a coherent statement on "polling data and local campaigns." Candidates were told that although most people did not believe that the NDP would form the next government, it was important for the party to have a strong presence in Parliament: "We are seen most importantly as defenders of the interests of ordinary Canadians. This indicates that we should be able to hold our own against arguments for a clean sweep to attain a new government. About one half of those people who now say they will vote Liberal are not firmly committed to this course. In contrast, over 75 per cent of PC intenders and over 70 per cent of New Democrats state that their intention is firm. In short, half of all Liberal voters may be persuaded to switch their allegiance. This group should be a target for NDP campaigns since Liberal intenders identify strongly with our positions on issues. Of those people who identify themselves in the long term as Liberals but do not plan to vote for that party in the coming election, as many intend to vote NDP as support the PCs. The Liberal voters (both soft and committed) like us because we stand up for ordinary people, they support our initiatives to protect social services, think the NDP helps those hard hit in bad economic times, believe the party makes sure corporations create jobs, think the NDP helps people against high interest rates, and fights to lower unemployment."

This analysis was crucial. The NDP did pick up fallen Liberals, and that made all the difference. The polling analysis also had this to say: "With the national view that the NDP's fortunes are at a low ebb our local campaigns will have to have a highly visible profile early on. This will show our workers and supporters right away that we are serious and in the game." Again, this was correct. Broadbent came out of the campaign starting gate almost before the flag was dropped and his early pace and high visibility began to have an effect on the naysayers. Before the disorganized Liberals or the early-stumbling Tories had got their campaigns on the road, Broadbent had made it clear that the NDP was in the fight to the end.

In summarizing the findings of the two Spring surveys, the party's national staff said that candidates and workers must "stress incumbent Members (of Parliament) as spokespeople for the concerns of ordinary Canadians and individuals who work hard for their communities." The report added that, "women are especially persuaded by our economic message. Overall people find that our economic message stressing standing up for ordinary people positively influences their vote." Beneath these last lines lay the struggle that was going on deep within the actual election strategy committee, made up of key members of Broadbent's staff and Caplan's staff. The struggle was over political reality and what Canadians would really accept from the mouths of New Democrats. There were a number of players, including Broadbent's press secretary, Rob Mingay, the leader's executive assistant, Bill Knight, and two of Caplan's staff, Julie Mason and Dennis Young — but the real players were Broadbent and Caplan themselves. They were different political animals. Broadbent still believed in preaching "full employment" and the forming of a New Democrat government. Caplan was not much interested in economics or the pretence of gaining power. He had worked for Lewis during his years as Ontario's NDP leader and in three provincial campaigns Lewis had never said the NDP would form the next government.

On top of the basic differences in the political and ideological nature of the two men, there was the awful atmosphere of pending disaster that pervaded the regular meetings. It seemed that almost every time they met, there was a new Gallup Poll out showing the NDP at rock bottom, between 11 and 13 per cent. One of the participants remembers: "It was such a terrible year. There was endless groping to get us back in the game. Today, it was more passion, tomorrow, it was more leader's tours, the next day it was more TV. It was a year of endless pain, of endless blows — and Broadbent took them all, from Hamilton, to Notley, to Blakeney, to Anguish, to Laxer." The election strategy group did not agree for a long time. "It was very tense," said a participant. "At times, people in the group were not speaking to each other, and the arguments were always held in the light of an ever worsening picture." Another said: "It was all going to ratshit, an endless escalator on the way down. No one was paying attention; we were becoming inconsequential. Every one per cent in the opinion polls meant another 100,000 voters lost. We were losing them by the month." Part of the tension grew out of the fact that there was still an inability to face facts, to admit that the NDP campaign would have to be different this time if the party was going to survive. All Caplan would say was: "Denying the self-evident is not helpful. If you treat reporters with some candor, if you acknowledge your problems, they will take you more seriously. Clearly, there have been people in the party who did not agree with that." At times, there were those who wondered if the NDP could actually pull itself out of the slough of despond, but in the end the rush of events — Trudeau's resignation, the coronation of Turner, and some signs of Liberal revival — served to concentrate the minds and stiffen the spines. The polls themselves had a critical effect, eventually burning into the reluctant traditionalists the realization that a strategy of "limited goals" had to be worked out. One of the most forceful arguments put forward by the initial proponents of a limited-goals-strategy was that Broadbent himself was respected by voters, whatever their political view, and he was respected most for talking straight. But if the leader and his incumbent MPs went out into the country talking about forming a government, let alone a majority government, the people would know that, "he was not telling the truth, not telling it straight." That, immediately, would diminish his credibility and take away one of his strongest assets.

The final, confidential memorandum that went from campaign director Caplan to the NDP campaign team was a curious mixture of realism and soft soap. Left out entirely were the nine "disadvantages" that had been so fearlessly enunciated in the strategic overview document just a month earlier. Instead, Caplan announced cheerfully in the second document, dated July 5, that "we face the campaign with much optimism." He went on: "The media and public reaction to the victory of John Turner presents an unanticipated opportunity for our party. Hardly anyone — not even Conservatives and Liberals — can explain what differentiates Mr. Turner from Mr. Mulroney. Self-satisfied business people publicly acknowledge that they are the real winners whichever man wins the election. Cartoonists and columnists across Canada have had a field day poking fun at the Chin and the Twin, Bobbsey Twins of Bay Street, the Corporate Clones, Brian Turner and John Mulroney. In other words, we begin with an immediate credibility when we assert that *they* are on the side of the privileged few, and *we* are on the side of the rest of Canadians. That's what this campaign is all about." The theme was that only the NDP could represent the ordinary Canadian. There was no mention of forming a government and no mention of making Canada once again a land of full employment. Instead, Caplan wrote: "Few expect us to form a government. We are admired because we can be counted on to fight for ordinary Canadians, not because we are expected to implement certain policies. We are respected because we are seen to be fighters for, not planners of." On the question of employment, he said: "Many voters are concerned, even anxious about their kids' practical futures, i.e., education and jobs. They believe we understand and share their concerns and they can count on us to be on their side." There was nothing like: "they can count on us to find them jobs."

Caplan went on to deal with the survival issue and how it could be turned into a positive element in the campaign platform. "Canadians don't want the NDP to disappear from the national scene. Whatever their political views, a significant number believe that our role as advocate for the under-privileged, as conscience of the nation, help make this a more decent country. Many Canadians, particularly in areas of our traditional strength, would be dismayed if they woke one day after the election to learn that the NDP had inadvertently been decimated. This is an important but subtle strength of the national party, and careful thought must be given to how it can be used in the campaign." That any NDP campaign official could even, in a roundabout fashion, suggest the party could be decimated in the 1984 campaign was an achievement in itself. Soft soap there was, but also a touch of realism. Caplan went on to ram home what the main message should be: "Ordinary Canadians need a voice in Parliament speaking up for their desire to have a fairer and more secure future. That voice will be ours: the New Democrats will speak on their behalf. It is *us* versus *them*. They know that John Turner and Brian Mulroney can't be trusted to be naturally on their side. So they need us to press the next government to act on their behalf."

The national director had been one of those who fought to keep specific economic issues out of the election manifesto, and instead to talk about things that were in the humanitarian or populist mainstream. In his charge to the troops, Caplan made it clear — if only in code words — that specificity was out, particularly on the question of the economy and jobs. The NDP had failed for too many years to win converts through its economic ideology, and this wasn't the time to start trying that again. It seemed that the campaign die had been cast. In fact, the argument over specificity and full employment rumbled on for weeks right into the campaign and beyond. The friction between the national leader and the national campaign director continued as Broadbent held out and Caplan kept chipping away at what he considered to be the unrealistic façade of old deal New Democrat politics. In fact, early in the campaign, Caplan became so concerned that he actually wrote a formal letter to Broadbent telling him to stop talking about full employment. But despite these continuing differences, the New Democrats managed to look as if they had no internal troubles at all. The national send-off was brilliantly devised by Broadbent to take place on Bay Street. While Mulroney, supremely confident that everything would unfold as it should, cruised through the country saying nothing of substance, and Turner tried to put a campaign team together, Broadbent was off at a furious pace, hammering away at the theme that only the New Democrats were different and offered a choice from the Bay Street world of the Conservative and Liberal leaders. In his kick-off speech on July 16, Broadbent used gentle sarcasm to effect in describing to the country what they had in Mulroney and Turner. "I have to admit that I did look closely and find some differences between John and Brian. One is a corporate lawyer from Bay Street, the other a corporate lawyer from St. James Street. One was a director of the Canadian Imperial Bank of Commerce, the second largest bank in Canada, the other was a director of Credit Foncier, another billion dollar financial institution. One was a corporate lawyer of Canadian Pacific, the second largest corporation in Canada, the other was corporate president of the Iron Ore Company of Canada, a branch plant resource company. And that's where the differences stop." Broadbent made a point that the country was faced with clones: "John Turner says he is a fresh face with a new plan. But he is really a recycled man with a recycled plan and a recycled cabinet — the only significant change is there are fewer women in Turner's cabinet than in Trudeau's last. Brian Mulroney also says he offers a new face and a change of direction for Canadians. But all he offers are platitudes, not policies. There is no choice between the corporate twins...they share the same vision of the world, the same view from the executive suites on the 45th floor, and they share the same reliance on the unfair policies that benefit the privileged few at the expense of ordinary Canadians. Looking down from the 45th floor, they can't see the ordinary men and women on the streets below. Looking down from the 45th floor, they promise even more tax breaks to the corporate few who share the offices on the 45th floor. And they deliver. Following Mulroney's advice, Lalonde, endorsed by Turner last Monday, gave the corporations additional millions — promising recovery. Well, their friends on the 45th floor did get the benefits; profits increased by more than 80 per cent last year — unemployment, however, remained at 1.5 million."

Broadbent went on to make another major speech in Vancouver laying out what he would do to the tax system in order to bring the so-called 45th floor down to street level: "It is no accident that the history of the development of democratic government has also been the history of who and in what manner the public treasury is controlled. The distribution of wealth in our society demonstrates fundamentally the type of society a government wants to see for its citizens; what kind of growth it wants and who is to pay for it. For me, the taxation system is an extremely powerful instrument to be used with care and foresight. It is probably the most important public instrument in developing a sense of fairness and co-operation." Broadbent proposed immediate implementation of a 20 per cent minimum tax for Canadians earning over $50,000. They made up only two per cent of those filing returns, but the number who were paying no tax at all had gone up from 300 to over 8,000 since the mid '70s. Days earlier, during the English-language television debate between the three leaders, Conservative leader Mulroney had surprisingly agreed with Broadbent that there was a need for more equity in the tax system, especially relating to high-income earners who paid no tax. Neither Mulroney nor Turner ever substantially came to grips with what the tax would be. In contrast, Broadbent has based his documented proposal on what U.S. Tax officials call the "alternative minimum tax." When laid out in detail in a Vancouver speech, the issue made headlines again. Broadbent grabbed the attention of the electorate with this proposal and his generally outstanding performance in the TV debates.

Broadbent's proposals for tax reform, however, were much more than just a slap at the rich. By mid-campaign, he had developed them into a rational program to help small business which, he argued, would also reduce unemployment. In a speech to the Winnipeg Chamber of Commerce on August 10, he talked about the essential role of small business in creating new jobs, in cooperation with a social democratic government: "Directing new opportunities to small business is a central element to our policy for new job opportunities for *ordinary Canadians*." (There was that phrase again). "The government of Manitoba had led the way by using its jobs fund to promote small business. The key here is co-operation between government and small business working together to benefit the community." Manitoba's results were, indeed, impressive. Unemployment had dropped to eight per cent, well below the national average. The province had had the largest decrease in business bankruptcies, down 17.9 per cent compared to 4.7 per cent nationally, 42 per cent of the labor force worked for small businesses, and in recent years this sector had been the major source of new jobs for Canadians. Between 1975 and 1982, businesses with fewer than 20 employees produced 86.4 per cent of the new growth in jobs. On the other hand, businesses with more than 100 employees lost jobs, 6.1 per cent in the same period. Broadbent argued that small business was much more accountable to the communities, particularly in relation to investing their earnings back into the region in which they operated. Yet this sector of the economy had been denied by government the opportunity to realize its full potential. The discrimination was easy to see, Broadbent told his audience of Manitoba businessmen. Loan rates to small business were three per cent higher than larger corporations. Eighty per cent of the corporate tax breaks went to the largest 0.5 per cent of corporations. To change this situation, Broadbent proposed lower and more stable interest rates, coupled with a tax on speculators to move rates lower. There should also be amendments to the Bank Act to provide lending rates to small business that compared with those offered big corporations. He suggested that the Federal Business Development Bank should provide more risk and venture capital for small business, and act as a clearing house for all small business programs.

The NDP reached the midpoint of the campaign in remarkable condition, considering it was still, in reality, a divided camp. Success fed on itself, and while many observers gave Caplan the main credit for creating what looked like a small miracle, Broadbent was the key to success. In the months leading up to the campaign, he had shown himself to be a man of quite remarkable fortitude and courage, enduring all the slings and arrows of outrageous fortune, including a painful back condition which necessitated surgery and might have finished off a man less psychologically sound. As Caplan himself put it: "He picked himself up off the ground, was thrilled with parts of the strategy, and revived himself in a way I would not have thought possible. I give him full marks for the way he came out fighting."

In a campaign that was basically dull and featureless because of the early collapse of the Liberal effort, the New Democrats' fight for survival became a real story. From the outset, the media — particularly CBC television — were more than fair in covering what was a minority party that did not even pretend any longer that it might form the next government. Nothing was more illustrative of this than Broadbent's participation as an equal in the television debates. There was never any question it would be anything else. "That Broadbent was on television as an equal with Mulroney and Turner was a victory in itself," Caplan said, "and he did wonderfully because he had a clear message to put across." The surprising substance and momentum of the NDP campaign was reflected in the reporting of the country's leading journalists who only weeks earlier had been prepared to write off the party, and even to consign it to history. Charlotte Montgomery of The Globe and Mail reported from Ottawa: "Whatever may lie ahead in the unpredictable weeks before September, at least the campaign has lost its nightmare qualities. There is no talk of forming a government and little more than hope that perhaps some seats might be taken from the competition. But there is also no talk of doing so poorly that the NDP loses its standing as an official party. By all that is politically sound, the NDP should be slogging grimly along, outspent as usual by the Liberals and the Conservatives, and burdened under the massive weight of polls that put the party at a record low when the election was called. It was a desperate scenario, a reminder that there were some who were convinced only a year ago that Mr. Broadbent should not be fighting this third campaign of his leadership. But by the end of the last week (August 4), NDP officials were shaking their heads in delighted wonderment. The legendary federal Liberal machine was in disarray, four hours of summer television had presented the NDP Leader to the public that appears to have admired his performance and, more importantly, not to have been taken with Prime Minister John Turner's behavior. Even the mechanically perfect organization brought to Conservative leader Brian Mulroney's campaign by Ontario's Big Blue Machine had ground its gears at least once. It was enough in those first nervous weeks to reassure the NDP'S core voters and to bring in a flood of requests to have Mr. Broadbent visit ridings where the local workers had not been clamoring loudly for his presence."

A week after the television debates, a CTV poll put the NDP at 17 per cent — 600,000 voters won back, Glory Be. Said one campaign organizer: "There was one magic moment in time when Turner was quite discredited and Mulroney was still seen as a huckster...and we were in the middle of it." A Gallup Poll of August 18 gave the New Democrats 18 per cent of the popular vote, a standing confirmed by a CROP poll taken between August 14 and 19. This survey indicated also that voters were deserting the Liberals in large numbers, with a significant number of them going to the NDP. Yet despite good news from the front and in the opinion samplings, the campaign still ran, just underneath the surface, on the ragged edges of internal dissent. There were those who had what might be called vaulting ambition — take the New Democrats through the 20 per cent barrier and on past the staggering Liberals into second place. Anything was possible, but to those who saw this as a natural goal, there were still two grave concerns: first, the leader persisted in talking policy when he should be concentrating on politics; second, the Tory flood was threatening to reach the edges of key NDP seats. As the strategists reached out for what in the end would be unattainable, their grasp failed them, their intellect froze and their fragile unity broke. "We did not know what to say," remembers one. "We somehow could not devise the next clever move, the next important slogan. Together, we did not develop the next stage. And on camera, we had begun to slip. There were television clips of forestry and shipbuilding, but we were meant to be running on politics."

Three weeks before voting day there were serious internal rows between the two party camps, one on Broadbent's campaign plane, and the other at election headquarters. All one participant would say, in retrospect, was that "heavy influences were brought in to tell Ed long distance that he was on the wrong track." But while the campaign was threatening to fracture, the media kept on reporting that the NDP was on a roll. "We disguised what was happening," said one organizer. "We kept it hidden from the media, we led them astray..." Then, on August 22, came the bombshell. Caplan decided that the Tory flood had become so strong it was going to sweep away New Democrats. The only way to stop this happening was to admit there was a Tory tidal wave and warn voters how important it was to have New Democrats elected. In a confidential directive from "the National Campaign Director" to candidates and campaign managers, Caplan said: "The shape of the battle is now clear. The Conservatives will pound away at every one of our good seats, insisting that a vote for the New Democrats is a wasted vote. They'll say your riding needs someone on the government side in order to have influence, to get government hand-outs, to get in on the gravy train... We must reply strongly to this pitch. Unless we counter attack, it has a superficial persuasiveness." Then came the stunner: "We agree the Conservatives are likely to have a large majority, maybe even a huge majority. There is no point in pretending about minority government any longer, but we can take advantage of the perception of a potential Tory landslide. Do you trust someone like Brian Mulroney and 200 Tory MPs to act in the interests of ordinary Canadians? Do you trust that they won't cut back on social services? Won't you trust the next government more if it has people like Ed Broadbent and your candidate in Parliament to keep those Tories honest?" Caplan went on to instruct the party's candidates to tell the waverers, the potential switchers, "so instead of wasting your vote by voting New Democrat, you're making it really count because the more votes for us, the stronger our voice will be for you." It was a masterful, although highly controversial, pitch. For some the voltage was too much. The national campaign director had admitted the Tories were going to win big, maybe very big. The memorandum containing this confession and the strategy to stop the Tories at the NDP door got into the hands of the media. Not only that, Broadbent had not been consulted about the final switch in strategy. The memorandum was simply sent to his campaign plane.

At first, there was no reaction from Broadbent's staff. Either they did not have time to read the memorandum properly or the implications of it did not sink in. NDP campaign commercials were already admitting tacitly there was going to be a large Tory victory, but when the Caplan memorandum leaked out, Broadbent was confronted by reporters wanting to know if he agreed there was a massive Tory tide running through the country. Just like admitting that full employment and an NDP government were things of the past, Broadbent found it virtually impossible to admit publicly in the final 10 days of an election campaign that the party he opposed the most was going to win a massive victory. The sparks flew once more, but Caplan was undeterred. He gave an interview to Canadian Press elaborating on his position. He said that the Tories had stepped up their advertising campaign in western Canada where the NDP drew its greatest support, and were hoping to knock off the party's 25 western incumbents one by one. Brutally frank, as usual, Caplan said the NDP was not asking for the balance of power in a minority government. A majority of voters would hate to see a third party with such power. All New Democrats wanted was a chance to play their traditional role of keeping the other parties honest. Once again, he had scaled down the target.

In his final speech of the campaign, Broadbent made no mention of the huge Tory tide. Instead, he continued to talk about the NDP's momentum, buoyed by another poll that put the New Democrats at 21 per cent. He also returned to his theme of the Bay Street twins, and how they could not be trusted to look after ordinary Canadians: "What about the voice of Bay Street — John Turner and Brian Mulroney? The voice of Bay Street has been dancing around the concerns of Canadians on jobs, equality for women, fair taxes, social programs and nuclear disarmament. John Turner and Brian Mulroney have spent this campaign finding new ways of avoiding the issues. They have created the Bay Street shuffle." In particular, he went after Mulroney on tax reform: "When I asked Mr. Mulroney in the television debate if he supported a minimum tax on the wealthy, he said 'The rich should pay handsomely.' But since the debate, his party has denied this is Conservative policy." And, in a final prediction and with a thumb to his nose at his campaign director, Broadbent concluded: "More Canadians than ever before are indicating they plan to vote for what they want, instead of simply for what they can get...There are going to be more New Democrats than ever before in the House of Commons after September the 4th."

Of course, that did not happen. Broadbent took his 30 seats and made the most of it, saying the New Democrats would be "the real opposition" to the Tories in the new Commons. What he did not say was that fortune had favored the brave. In many seats the NDP won, its popular vote was down from 1980. In the end, the Liberal collapse evened itself out, resulting in new NDP seats in Ontario and losses in the West. One NDP insider described it all as "longterm pain for short-term gain." But Ian McKinnon of Decima Research Ltd., which polled for the Tories, admitted publicly a month later that Caplan's strategy predicting a Tory landslide had saved NDP seats. Ironically, the same strategy had helped Turner win Quadra.

For Caplan, however, that was not good enough. Determined to leave his position as National Director, he announced he would depart at the end of the year. After 15 elections over 50 years, during which neither the NDP nor its CCF predecessor had ever received more than 20 per cent of the vote, Caplan said, "The party has to say it's time to ask what went wrong." As he himself admitted, there are more than a few people in the party who were relieved to see him go. But without Caplan, and the resilient Broadbent, there might well have been in the end no official NDP to ask what went wrong.

CHAPTER 3

WHO SHOT J.T.? — THE MEDIA COVERAGE

During a national election, relatively few Canadians are actively engaged in the campaign and thereby have firsthand information about candidates and policies. The vast majority rely on the news media for facts and opinions, and even when they receive information from family or friends, the original source may well have been the media. It is reasonable to assume therefore that the way in which the media report an election campaign will have some influence on people's voting decisions and thus on the result. But the key phrase here is "some influence". Voters may also be influenced by family tradition, regional preferences, group loyalties, political advertising, direct mail propaganda and other factors. The impact of media coverage on a campaign must vary from voter to voter and in many cases it may be filtered and used to confirm prior judgement; in other words, contrary evidence is reinterpreted or simply ignored by the voter. Nevertheless, the news media devote substantial resources to election coverage, and journalists worry about the quality of their work and its effect on the democratic process. After every campaign, there is an internal debate and inquest: were they fair in their treatment of the candidates and parties, or did bias creep into their coverage; did they focus too closely on the leaders and ignore the "real issues"; did they, in short, provide the information the voters needed to make a responsible decision on how to vote? Following the 1984 election, for example, The Centre for Investigative Journalism, a national organization of journalists, organized conferences in Ottawa and in Montreal to discuss Who Shot J.T.? The consensus seemed to be that John Turner shot himself in the foot by his ineptness as a campaigner, although Bob Hepburn, Ottawa bureau chief for the Toronto Star, the largest paper in the country, complained that the reporters had been tougher on Turner than on Brian Mulroney: "With Turner, we always went after him as a group. We smelled blood, and we attacked. With Mulroney, we attacked at the end, but at the end people had already made up their minds." On the other hand, Douglas Fisher, the syndicated columnist and broadcaster who was formerly an MP, argued persuasively that the voters had better access to information from all sources in the 1984 election than ever before. There were disagreements among the journalists also on other questions of coverage. Murray Goldblatt, formerly Ottawa Bureau Chief for The Globe and Mail and now a Professor of Journalism at Carleton University in Ottawa, thought it disgraceful that the media had paid so little attention to policy issues. But Elly Alboim, the CBC's manager of campaign coverage, replied that policy issues were not crucial in the election, and wondered whether journalists had a right to impose policy debates on candidates who might have a different agenda to present to the electorate.

These debates within the media occur in different forms among politicians and among interested voters. Politicians often feel wounded by media coverage of their campaigns; even when they win, they feel they have done it despite critical journalists, and they worry about the power of the media to distort their message or to impose priorities upon them. Members of the public who follow politics are often ready to cite example of bias or at least inaccuracy in the news media, and sometimes to suggest that the media were mainly responsible for the defeat of their candidate or party. The problem with all these discussions about the performance of the media in covering campaigns is that they are based on guesses rather than on evidence. The purpose of this chapter is to provide evidence on just how selected organs of the media covered the campaign of 1984. The goal is not to say how the media affected the outcome of the election because that is beyond our power; it is to measure what can be measured with reasonable accuracy, and to suggest a few conclusions.

It is customary to say that TV has replaced newspapers as the major source of news for most Canadians, and this is probably true if one thinks of news in terms of headlines and brief bulletins about the great events of the day. But an election has many facets that are better covered by newspapers. For examples, while TV can focus with great effect on the campaigns of the party leaders, the battle is decided in 282 constituencies and each of these can be covered in depth by the local newspaper; TV can show the style and drama of politics, but it usually leaves to newspapers the thoughtful discussion of issues; TV journalists are allowed a certain latitude in interpreting the news they report, but it is newspaper columnists and editors who offer frank opinions on events and give advice to the voters. In short, newspaper coverage of an election is, or should be, longer, broader and deeper than that offered by TV. For these reasons, newspaper coverage of the campaign was chosen as the major focus for this study. Seven newspapers, each a leader in its market, were selected for examination: The Sun in Vancouver, the Free Press in Winnipeg, the Star in Toronto, the Gazette and La Presse in Montreal, the Chronicle-Herald in Halifax, and the National Edition of The Globe and Mail which is edited in Toronto but printed in centres across the country and distributed nationally. Every journalistic item dealing with the election for every day of the campaign was clipped, analysed and coded — 5,609 items in all, including news reports, analyses of the news, articles by columnists, editorials expressing the opinion of the paper, photographs and cartoons. From this mass of data should emerge a comprehensive picture of just how these papers covered the election. The seven are not of course representative of the press in Canada — most papers are smaller and have fewer resources to devote to coverage — but they are widely read and influential in their markets. To some extent, they set the standards for the press. Let us now see how they performed.

The first test is to measure the space they devoted to all forms of election coverage during the 57 days of the campaign.

TABLE 1
Extent of Coverage

	V.Sun	W.FP	T.Star	M.Gaz.	M.LP	H.C-H	G & M
Total edit space available (column ins.)	191,903	157,365	281,109	168,836	301,488	167,868	198,694
Space devoted to election coverage (column ins.)	15,701	13,214	22,704	15,059	18,793	12,569	15,702
Percent of space devoted to election coverage	8.18	8.40	8.08	8.92	6.23	7.49	7.90

The figures are not directly comparable as the Toronto Star and the Montreal La Presse publish seven days a week and the others only six and as the length and width of columns varies from paper to paper, and in fact from news page to feature page within each newspaper. But it is apparent that all the papers devoted very substantial amounts of space to covering the election. In fairness to The Globe and Mail, it should be remembered that we are measuring the National Edition, as compared with the major hometown editions of the others. Had we measured the Toronto edition of the Globe and found more coverage of local ridings, the total of space would have increased. But in general the editors of the English-language papers might almost have been working to a formula, so close were they in deciding what proportion of total editorial space to devote to election coverage. As the largest paper in terms of "newshole" — that is, total

TABLE 2
Breadth of Coverage
(Percentages) *

	V.Sun	W.FP	T.Star	M.Gaz.	M.LP	H.C-H	G & M
News items	65.9	72.9	73.6	65.6	78.2	82.6	68.3
Backgrounder/analysis	7.8	3.4	7.1	7.9	2.1	2.7	4.2
Column/comment	15.7	11.6	8.0	14.8	11.2	1.3	12.6
Editorial opinion	5.0	4.2	3.4	4.3	2.8	3.5	6.5
Photos **	1.8	3.0	2.9	2.8	3.5	9.4	4.7
Cartoons	3.8	4.8	4.9	4.6	2.0	0.6	3.7
Number of items	(739)	(768)	(1035)	(581)	(1043)	(631)	(812)

*In all the tables percentages may not add to exactly 100 due to rounding.
**Photos illustrating a news report or article are included under those headings; photos counted here are those standing alone as a separate editorial item.

editorial space available — the French-language La Presse was able to commit a smaller proportion to the election , but still to provide more coverage than any other paper except the Toronto Star. The next step is to examine how the space available for the election was divided between news, comment, and opinion.

The Halifax Chronicle-Herald is one of the smaller papers in the sample, but even so it is noticeable that its readers got short measure in the way of commentary and analysis. While the distribution of the various types of coverage varied in the other papers, that may be accounted for in part by editorial style. Where reporters are given more freedom to provide background and explanation in their news reports, there is less need for special articles to put news into perspective. This probably explains the distribution in La Presse because it is the style of French Canadian journalism to allow reporters to include analysis in their reports. But certainly it would be hard to argue from these figures that readers were deprived of news, comment or opinion, with the possible exception of those of the Chronicle-Herald.

Newspapers obtain their election coverage from a variety of sources: staff reporters, feature writers and commentators; Canadian Press, the national wire service co-operatively owned and run by the papers; other news and feature services offering editorial material for sale; and in some cases, news services provided by the newspaper group or chain to which they belong — for example, the Southam News service which provides to its papers news and commentary written by staff correspondents in Canada and abroad. There is no ideal mix, but it is generally accepted that readers are best served when papers compete to cover the news with their own staffs, and rely on Canadian Press and other services as backups and as the source occasionally of other views and opinions about the news.

TABLE 3
Source of Coverage
(Percentages)

	V.Sun	W.FP	T.Star	M.Gaz.	M.LP	H.C-H	G & M
Staff	66.2	37.8	66.7	44.8	59.6	50.8	70.2
CP	14.5	49.1	17.5	23.8	9.1	44.7	19.0
Others	19.3	13.1	15.8	31.4	31.3	4.5	10.8
Number of items	(739)	(768)	(1035)	(581)	(1043)	(631)	(812)

Two of the papers in the sample, the Vancouver Sun and the Montreal Gazette, are members of the Southam group and have access to the extensive service of news and commentary filed daily from Ottawa. This supplements the work of staff writers and reduces dependence on Canadian Press. As the paper with the largest circulation in the country, the Toronto Star has the resources to rely mainly on its own staff, and in fact it sells the work of its featured commentators, such as columnist Richard Gwyn, to other papers across Canada. La Presse also is a large paper with an extensive staff, but the reason it relies on Canadian Press so much less than others in the sample is probably that it focuses on politics in Quebec and is less interested in news from other parts of Canada. The Globe and Mail is the flagship of the Thomson chain and seems to enjoy freedom from the severe budgetary controls imposed by head office on less famous and fortunate papers. In any event, the Globe was able to rely mainly on its own staff for election coverage. The Winnipeg Free Press, also a Thomson paper, was not so fortunate; with limited staff resources and little in the way of a Thomson news service on which to draw, it had to rely very heavily on CP. The Halifax Chronicle-Herald divided the task of coverage between its own staff and CP, and provided only a little of news and commentary from other sources, partly because it is an independent paper without access to a group service.

The next question to consider is from where the news came, in the sense of where it happened.

TABLE 4
Origin of Items
(Percentages)

	V.Sun	W.FP	T.Star	M.Gaz.	M.LP	H.C-H	G & M
Ottawa	14.5	17.3	20.0	23.8	5.8	17.0	21.3
B.C.	55.9	7.9	11.5	9.3	5.6	8.6	8.4
Alta.	2.2	3.1	2.6	2.6	1.5	1.3	1.8
Sask.	1.1	1.6	2.3	1.0	0.7	2.1	1.6
Man.	0.8	32.2	2.8	1.7	1.4	2.7	3.2
Ont.	7.8	12.9	35.9	14.8	8.6	13.3	32.9
Que.	6.2	11.2	11.2	35.8	64.2	10.3	12.7
N.B.	0.4	1.6	0.9	0.7	0.4	1.3	0.9
N.S.	1.5	0.4	2.2	2.4	1.1	36.0	2.6
P.E.I.	0.1	0.8	0.6	0.7	0.1	1.1	0.4
Nfld.	0.7	0.1	1.1	0.3	0.2	1.1	1.5
Yukon/NWT	0.3	0.4	0.3	0.3	0.2	0.0	0.2
Other *	8.6	10.2	8.6	6.5	10.3	5.4	12.5
Number of items	(739)	(768)	(1035)	(581)	(1043)	(631)	(812)
Percent. from home province	55.9	32.2	35.9	35.8	64.2	36.0	32.9

* No specific location mentioned, or in a few cases from abroad.

The importance of Ottawa as a source of news and commentary about a national election is hardly surprising, but it is interesting to note that the French-language La Presse paid far less attention to the capital than the English-language papers. Its focus on Quebec seems to confirm the view that even in national politics, Quebec is not a province like the others. British Columbia also is often thought of as a far-away land wrapped up in its own concerns, and this finds support in the data. It needs to be remembered, however, that both Quebec and British Columbia had special roles in the campaign as homebases for Mulroney and Turner, and for them a proportion of local coverage was also national coverage. The other five papers were remarkably consistent in the proportions of attention they gave to their home provinces and to the rest of Canada: the coverage was well spread, with little evidence of parochialism. Interestingly, the Star which emphasizes in its advertising its commitment to Metro Toronto provided more coverage from all regions than the National Edition of The Globe and Mail.

In all those thousands of reports and commentaries filling hundreds of columns, who were the papers covering? The national party leaders are of course the figures of greatest interest and it is often complained that the press focuses on them to the exclusion of other candidates. The following table analyses each item of coverage to see in what proportion the leaders were in fact the "principal actors" — that is, the focus of the item — and how this attention was divided among the leaders.

TABLE 5
Leaders as Principal Actors
(Percentages)

	V.Sun	W.FP	T.Star	M.Gaz.	M.LP	H.C-H	G & M
Turner	13.8	8.5	15.5	16.5	14.2	13.3	17.4
Mulroney	7.8	6.3	13.7	10.3	11.1	10.3	11.1
Broadbent	4.9	3.8	8.6	6.7	4.4	7.0	8.3
Other	73.5	81.4	62.2	66.5	70.3	68.4	73.2
Number of items	(739)	(768)	(1035)	(581)	(1043)	(631)	(812)

It turns out that in all the papers the leaders were the centre of attention in only a minority of items, ranging from 37.8 per cent in the Star to only 18.6 per cent in the Free Press. Obviously, many other people enjoyed exposure as "Principal Actors" in the coverage.

In every paper, there were more items which Turner was the principal figure (796) than there were items which highlighted Mulroney (579), but as we shall see later, all publicity is not necessarily good publicity, at least during an election campaign. The fact that Turner was prime minister no doubt explains some of the attention. He had also just returned from private life to politics and in that sense was more newsworthy than his opponent, and required closer scrutiny. The NDP was so low in the opinion polls at the outset of the campaign that it was feared that Broadbent might be unable to attract media coverage, thus helping to fulfill the predictions that the party would suffer a devastating defeat. These figures show, however, that while Broadbent received less attention than Turner and Mulroney, he was still treated as the leader of a substantial party. In summary, the national leaders received fair shares in terms of their standing and newsworthiness when we count the number of items of coverage. But items may be long or short, displayed on the front page or buried inside. They may have a big headline or a small one, an accompanying picture or not. How they are presented to the readers determines to some extent what attention they will

TABLE 6
Attention Score of Items About Leaders
(Percentages)

	Turner	Mulroney	Broadbent
High	33.6	33.1	19.4
Medium	45.6	48.0	54.2
Low	20.8	18.8	27.5
Number of items	(796)	(579)	(350)

receive. Therefore, an "attention score" was devised to measure the prominence of every item. (1)

We have already noted that there were more items about Turner than about Mulroney. These figures show that the additional items were spread over the range of "attention" categories, thereby confirming that Turner did in fact receive substantially more coverage than his opponent. Items about Broadbent tended to be grouped in the low and medium ranges; there were relatively few which would have commanded great attention.

Another way to analyse political content is to look at the party affiliation of the principal actor in every story. This takes us far beyond the party leaders and enables us to see broadly the shares of space — in terms of numbers of items —obtained by all Liberals, Conservatives and New Democrats who appeared as principal actors in items of coverage.

TABLE 7
Party Affiliation of All Principal Actors
(Percentages)

	V.Sun	W.FP	T.Star	M.Gaz.	M.LP	H.C-H	G & M
Lib.	29.6	27.9	32.9	35.6	36.9	32.5	38.2
Cons.	16.2	19.3	23.1	20.0	24.5	25.7	20.8
NDP	10.1	9.2	10.4	9.1	6.5	12.2	11.2
Ind.	1.1	0.7	0.8	0.5	0.2	0.6	0.9
Libertarian	0.1	0.4	0.0	0.0	0.0	0.0	0.1
Communist	0.7	0.7	0.1	0.5	0.1	0.2	0.2
Green	2.0	0.1	0.3	0.2	0.4	0.0	0.2
Rhino	1.4	1.4	1.0	1.5	1.2	1.0	0.7
No actor or party	38.8	40.3	34.4	32.6	30.2	27.8	27.7
Number of items	(739)	(768)	(1035)	(581)	(1043)	(631)	(812)

Liberals received far more coverage than Conservatives, 1,881 items as opposed to 1,210, again perhaps because they were the party of government; ministers make more news than their opposition critics, and MPs are better known than candidates seeking to win a seat. What is particularly noticeable in this table is the short thrift given to the minor parties. Among them, the Rhinos did best in coverage, presumably because they provided light relief during the campaign. Communists were barely visible, Libertarians even less so. The Greens who have become a significant force in Europe were only just making an appearance in Canadian election coverage, mainly in the Vancouver Sun probably because the ecology movement is stronger on the West coast than elsewhere.

We can turn now from content in terms of leaders and parties to content in terms of topics. To what extent were the papers reporting and commenting on policies and programs, and to what extent were they examining the processes of campaigning? Obviously, thousands of different subjects become news during a national election and an attempt to list and describe them all would be hopeless. For the purposes of analysis, it is necessary to group many topics under broad headings, and to spotlight those of particular interest. We can also group topics in categories — party issues and proposals, the political process, special coverage such as opinion polls, TV debates etc. — and measure how coverage was divided between these categories and what prominence each was given. Finally, we can recognize that many items cover more than one subject, so we can analyse each item by main and secondary topic.

TABLE 8
Issues Covered
(Percentages)

	Main Topic	Secondary Topic
Economy	21.5	23.9
National Unity	15.0	15.0
Peace/Defence	11.5	8.0
Women's Rights	11.2	15.9
Patronage	10.4	9.7
Unemployment	6.9	8.0
Tax Reform	5.4	5.3
Energy	4.2	2.7
Social	4.2	3.5
Change in Ottawa	3.8	4.4
Agriculture	2.7	0.9
U.S. Relations	1.2	0.9
Other Foreign Relations	1.2	0.9
Technology	0.8	0.9
Number of items	(1459)	(631)

Thus of 5,609 items analysed, 1,459, or 26 per cent, had a policy issue or proposal as its main topic. In all the rest of the coverage — almost three-quarters of the total — the main topic was something other than policy.

The figures make clear that Economic issues in general — a group which includes the budget deficit, the value of the dollar, party proposals to deal with economic problems and the cost of those proposals, and many other topics — dominated the policy discussions on the hustings, such as they were. The dominance becomes even more complete when we add the topics that might be considered to be Economic but have been counted separately because they seemed to be of special interest. According to opinion polls, unemployment was a major concern in the minds of the voters, and it received substantial coverage. Prior to the election, the Conservatives had made the cause of tax reform a major issue in the House of Commons, alleging abuse of artists, businessmen and others by the tax collectors, and promising change. It appears they were able to carry this issue into the campaign, attracting considerable attention. Agriculture is a major industry, but received little attention from the press, and the whole range of issues associated with Technology were scarcely noticed. After Economy, the group of issues receiving the most attention were those concerned with National Unity — reform of the constitution, bilingualism, multiculturalism, Quebec separatism, Western alienation, and others. These issues tended to be associated in the past with the former prime minister, Pierre Trudeau, and the country was said to be tired of them, but clearly they did not go away with Trudeau. Peace/Defence includes discussions on the role Canada should play in disarmament negotiations and also in military alliances such as NATO and Norad. The Liberal government's decision to allow the United States to test cruise missiles over Canadian territory had outraged the peace movements, but its impact as an issue in the election was muted because the Conservatives were agreement with the Liberals. The Conservatives put some emphasis on the campaign plank of improving relations with the United States, but this did not attract much coverage — and all other foreign relations were even less noticed. Women's Rights (including the abortion issue, although it is obviously of interest to men also) were a major subject for campaign discussion, almost certainly for the first time in a Canadian election. Social Issues include the question of universality —that is to say, should family allowances and old age pensions continue to be paid to all who qualify or restricted to those in need —the looming problem of financing private and public pensions, education and other topics across the board to capital punishment. They received relatively little attention, presumably because this was an election in which the candidates were promising to tighten belts rather than to introduce new programs. Patronage became an issue when Turner made a number of appointments to the Senate and to other public positions at the request of the outgoing prime minister, Trudeau. The media saw this as a scandalous example of Liberal porkbarrelling, and the Conservatives were quick to exploit it. Although Turner denied responsibility, insisting that he had no option but to carry out Trudeau's wishes in the matter, the issue continued to haunt him through the campaign, as the media coverage shows. Mulroney allowed in an unguarded moment that he might not be much different than the Liberals in giving and receiving patronage, but this did not seem to let the Liberals off the hook, and the subject received a large amount of coverage, far more for example than unemployment. One might argue that the topic was hugely overblown to the disadvantage of the Liberals, or one could say that patronage was of great interest and importance because it symbolized for the electorate the decay of the Liberal government and party and was associated with the issue of time-for-a-change in Ottawa.

The table of secondary topics shows that there were no "sleeper" issues in the sense that while not rating as high as primary topics, they showed up heavily as secondary topics for coverage. Indeed, Economic topics were again at the head of the table, emphasizing the dominance of these subjects among policy issues, and Women's Rights were in second place.

If we accept that the state of the economy was an issue advantageous to the Conservatives, it appears that they won the battle of the "agenda" in press coverage. National unity had previously been a Liberal issue, but in this election the Conservative leader was promising better representation to both Quebec and the West. The Liberals were on the defensive in Quebec following the retirement of their French-Canadian leader, Trudeau, and the choice of an anglophone from Toronto as his successor, and their credentials as nation builders had not for some years been accepted in the West. So national unity probably favored the Conservatives. The traditional Liberal leadership in social policy rang few bells in this election.

Issues, however, were not the principal interest of the media during the campaign. There were more items devoted to the political process during the campaign — that is to say, to the organizations and strategies of the parties, the boys (and now girls) in the smoke-filled rooms, the selection of candidates, and so on.

TABLE 9
Coverage of the Political Process
(Percentages)

	Main Topic	Secondary Topic
Lib. Party organization and campaign	28.5	33.4
Cons. Party org./camp.	19.8	16.6
NDP Party org./camp.	10.1	11.1
All other parties org./camp.	6.4	2.2
Other campaign items *	19.3	27.8
Candidate selection	15.9	8.9
Number of items	(2,193)	(501)

* Items covering the campaigns of more than one party, or covering campaign in general terms.

A total of 2,193 items, or 38.9 per cent, were about process rather than policy: to put it another way, they dealt with the machinery rather than the product. Among these reports and commentaries, by far the largest single group focused on the Liberal party, and indeed the state of the organization and the problems with Turner's campaign became major topics of discussion: the papers printed twice as many items on this topic as they did on all the Economic policy subjects. The Conservative party's organization and campaign received much less but still major attention: there were about twice as many items on this as on the whole issue of National Unity.

Journalists have themselves noticed the emphasis they placed on process in this campaign. One explanation is that political reporters have covered so many major events in recent years — general elections and national party conventions — that they know the players and the game better than ever before: a system that used to be opaque has become transparent and therefore easy to write about. Another view is that in this election, Process was in fact more important than Policy. Turner and Mulroney were both claiming to be new leaders at the head of new teams, and it was important to examine their claims and to assess their abilities as organizers and leaders: if the voters were demanding change in Ottawa, actions, styles and attitudes could count for more than policies and promises that might be forgotten after the election. We can look now at a third group of miscellaneous items that dealt with neither process nor policy in the usual sense. (Many of these items deal with topics of regional or local concern or matters that cannot be coded into any broad category, and they appear as "Other" in the table.)

These items constitute 35 per cent of all coverage. It is surely noteworthy that 14.5 per cent of these, or 5 per cent of all election items, had opinion polls — results, interpretation, criticism of polls, and so on — as their primary subject. Almost an equal number of items had polls as the secondary subject. Polls have obviously become a major component of election coverage. So have TV debates among the leaders: properly ignoring the fact that they are first brought to the public by a rival news medium, the press treats them as a major subject for

TABLE 10
Other Coverage
(Percentages)

	Main Topic
Opinion Polls	14.5
TV Debates	12.2
Campaign "blunders"	6.0
Media campaign coverage	3.1
Criticism of Turner	6.0
Criticism of Mulroney	6.0
Criticism of Broadbent	0.6
Criticism of Lib. party	4.0
Criticism of Cons. party	2.0
Criticism of NDP	0.6
Criticism of other parties	0.6
Quality of Leadership	0.6
Other	43.8
Number of items	(1957)

reporting and for commentary. For journalists, polls and TV debates perhaps have a similar attraction: polls are used mostly to report which party is ahead in the race; TV debates show the party leaders in direct combat and can be reported in terms of winners and losers. Campaign "blunders", or perceived blunders, became for the press a measure of their competence. Although the general impression is probably that Turner blundered more frequently than his opponent, this does not show up in the numbers of items directly critical of the leaders. They came out just about even — with Broadbent as the big winner because he attracted hardly any criticism. However, when the subject was criticism of the parties rather than the leaders, the Liberals suffered twice as badly as the Conservatives — and again, the NDP escaped almost unscathed.

We cannot now deduce from these results any bias in the coverage. Turner and Mulroney were treated with an even hand; as the party in power and in charge of patronage, the Liberal party may have attracted criticism simply by what it did, while the Conservative party, free from the responsibilities of office, had less to answer for; and Broadbent and the NDP perhaps were quite as blameless as it appears, or possibly received less critical scrutiny because they were not thought to be likely winners. The press, it will be noted, was not very active in reporting on its own performance in the campaign.

Quality of Leadership is included in this table only because it deserves some attention but does not fit elsewhere. Studies of previous elections have suggested that voters are influenced more by the leadership qualities of the candidates than by any other factor when deciding which party to support. It may have been the case again in this election with the media providing the ideas, information and images on which the voters made up their minds. But what is clear is that the press had little to say about leadership as a specific topic.

We have been looking at content in terms of numbers of items. Now let us look at the prominence given to some of the major issues using the "attention score" described above.

TABLE 11
Major Issues by Attention Scores
(Percentages)

	Economy	National Unity	Peace/ Defence	Women's Rights	Patronage
Low	18.5	24.7	24.6	33.8	30.6
Medium	50.0	45.7	44.4	45.0	48.7
High	31.5	29.7	31.0	21.2	21.0
Number of items	(314)	(219)	(171)	(160)	(152)

The figures confirm again the dominance of economic topics. There were not only more items about this range of subjects than about any other, but they tended to be presented in such a way as to command more attention than other subjects.

TABLE 12
Process by Attention Score
(Percentages)

	Lib. party org. and campaign	Cons. party org. and campaign	NDP party org. and campaign
Low	27.7	25.3	29.7
Medium	45.3	48.4	50.7
High	27.0	26.3	19.6
Number of items	(625)	(434)	(219)

This table suggests no significant difference in the display of items about the parties.

TABLE 13
Other Topics by Attention Score
(Percentages)

	Polls	TV Debates	Campaign Blunders	Criticism of Turner	Criticism of Mulroney
Low	25.3	26.7	21.8	26.1	22.6
Medium	41.8	39.2	51.3	42.9	47.0
High	33.0	34.2	26.9	31.1	30.4
Number of items	(285)	(240)	(119)	(119)	(115)

We have already noted that the papers printed about the same number of items criticizing Turner as criticizing Mulroney. We can now see that they were remarkably evenhanded in displaying these criticisms.

We have been examining coverage of subjects by all seven papers combined. Let us now look to see if the pattern of coverage was the same across the country, or if there were significant differences reflecting perhaps different regional interests and priorities.

TABLE 14
Major Policies and Proposals, by Paper
(Percentages)

	V.Sun	W.FP	T.Star	M.Gaz.	M.LP	H.C-H	G & M
Economy	26.3	20.8	26.2	25.9	33.1	33.1	31.8
Nat. Unity	16.3	22.2	15.9	19.0	33.1	14.8	13.4
Peace/Defence	18.6	20.8	15.0	13.8	8.9	17.6	16.6
Women's Rights	16.3	16.7	18.3	10.3	14.7	12.0	10.2
Patronage	12.4	13.2	13.7	17.2	8.9	13.3	19.1
Unemployment	10.1	6.3	10.9	13.8	5.3	9.2	8.9
Number of items	(127)	(144)	(202)	(116)	(225)	(142)	(157)

The Montreal Gazette printed fewer items on these major issues than the other papers, but obviously this was not a matter of regional priorities because La Presse, also of Montreal, paid more attention than all the other papers — with particular attention, not surprisingly, to National Unity. The pattern of coverage among the five other papers is sufficiently similar to be able to say that their agendas were national rather than regional or provincial. It is interesting to note, however, that The Globe and Mail was less interested than most papers in Women's Rights and more interested in the Patronage "scandals" — although it is possible that the pattern is affected by the fact that we are examining the National Edition with its emphasis on news likely to be of interest to business people.

TABLE 15
Major Process Items, by Paper
(Percentages)

	V.Sun	W.FP	T.Star	M.Gaz.	M.LP	H.C-H	G & M
Lib.Py.Org. and campaign	42.6	47.1	48.2	53.5	55.8	43.1	49.4
Con.Py.Org and campaign	34.8	31.2	34.0	28.4	34.0	43.1	32.1
NDP Py. Org. and campaign	22.6	21.7	17.8	18.1	10.2	13.8	18.5
Number of items	(155)	(135)	(247)	(116)	(235)	(144)	(243)

Apart from the Halifax Chronicle-Herald which managed by design or accident but with splendid impartiality to publish exactly the same number of items on both the major parties and their campaigns, the other papers were all far more interested in the Liberal party than its rivals.

TABLE 16
Other Major Items, by Paper
(Percentages)

	V.Sun	W.FP	T.Star	M.Gaz.	M.LP	H.C-H	G & M
Polls	38.9	31.9	26.8	28.3	28.2	25.3	22.6
TV Debates	22.1	21.3	23.4	23.2	27.6	18.1	29.9
Blunders	20.4	12.0	9.1	13.7	13.2	3.6	10.9
Criticism of Turner	6.2	10.6	12.0	14.5	10.3	10.8	18.3
Criticism of Mulroney	7.1	12.8	18.2	8.7	8.6	8.4	12.4
Criticism of Lib. party	3.5	6.4	7.2	8.7	9.8	19.3	4.4
Criticism of Cons. party	1.8	5.0	3.3	2.9	2.3	14.5	1.5
Number of items	(113)	(141)	(209)	(138)	(174)	(83)	(137)

The Toronto Star is a strongly Liberal newspaper and endorsed the party in this election. It may be no accident therefore that the percentage of its coverage critical of Mulroney was higher than that in any of the other papers. The Globe and Mail, on the other hand, is conservative in its editorial views, and endorsed the Conservative party in the election, and was more critical of Turner than of Mulroney. In dealing with the leaders, the other papers, with the exception of the Gazette, distributed their critical items more equally. But when it came to the parties, the Liberals were criticized more than the Conservatives in every paper, including the Star. In other areas, the pattern of coverage was similar in most of the papers.

The following table shows that all the papers gave more attention to process than to issues.

TABLE 17
Areas of Coverage, by Paper
(Percentages)

	V.Sun	W.FP	T.Star	M.Gaz.	M.LP	H.C-H	G & M
Issues	21.2	24.2	28.0	23.9	27.8	30.7	25.0
Process	40.6	37.6	35.6	37.2	41.4	40.9	40.6
Other	38.2	38.2	36.4	38.9	30.8	28.4	34.4
Number of items	(739)	(768)	(1035)	(581)	(1043)	(631)	(812)

The data so far has been obtained by objective measurement and analysis: that is to say, we have simply been recording facts. We turn now to a subjective analysis to attempt to assess the impact of election coverage on the readers. Obviously, readers can take different messages out of the same editorial item, depending on their own preconceptions, how carefully they read, and other factors. What will seem fair reporting to one reader will appear biased to another. So there is no reliable way to measure the impact of all the coverage on all the readers. Nevertheless, it is useful to look as objectively as possible at the content of the coverage to see how it was likely to impress the reasonable reader. Therefore, the researchers who read, measured and clipped all the editorial items concerning the election were asked to make a judgement about each: on reading it, would the average person obtain a favorable, unfavorable or neutral impression of the principal actor or party in the item? To ensure some consistency, the researchers individually first read and assessed a number of items and then compared notes and discussed standards they would use in the analysis.

We are not here measuring bias. A report may be accurate and fair and yet still leave the reader with an unfavorable impression of the principal actor or party concerned because that actor or party has done or said something of which the reader disapproves. Nevertheless, we would expect to find that the great majority of news reports and of news analyses are neutral in their impact. But editorials, columns and carto , are not necessarily intended to be neutral: they are often points of view desigr. l to leave the reader with a certain impression.

TABLE 18
Reader's Impression by Type of Item
(Percentage)

	News	News Background	Editorial	Column/ Comment	Cartoon	Photo
Neutral	90.9	80.9	48.1	54.4	20.7	94.9
Favorable	0.7	4.0	12.4	8.2	0.5	2.3
Unfavorable	3.7	5.4	33.5	31.6	74.7	2.3
Not applicable *	4.7	9.7	6.0	5.8	4.0	0.5
Number of items	(4082)	(277)	(233)	(603)	(198)	(216)

* No principal actor or party mentioned.

The table makes it clear that in discussing favorable and unfavorable coverage in news reports we are dealing with a very small percentage — less than 5 per cent. Most of the items that left an impression were those intended to do so, particularly the cartoons. Photographs standing alone were in the vast majority neutral, although there were a few that had a point to make. One of these no doubt was a picture of Turner in the Globe that, by a trick of lighting, appeared to show horns coming out of his head. Such featured pictures can upset the victim's keenest supporters, please his critics, and probably amuse most readers. It is questionable if they have a lasting impact on opinion unless they seem to dramatize an idea already broadly held if not fully acknowledged. For example, in the 1974 election, Conservative leader Robert Stanfield was shown dropping a football. The selection of the picture was unfair in the sense that Stanfield successfully caught the ball on several occasions. But it had point and impact because it appeared at a time when opinion was growing that Stanfield was in fact fumbling his campaign. A picture showing Turner fumbling might have had the same impact, but one showing him with horns was too amusing to be severely damaging: while many people may have thought him an unimpressive campaigner, few would identify him with the devil.

TABLE 19
Readers' Impressions of Actors and Parties
(Percentages)

	Turner	Mul-roney	Broad-bent	Other Libs.	Other Cons.	Other NDP	Lib. party	Cons. party
Neutral	73.4	80.7	92.6	90.6	95.0	96.6	65.6	86.7
Favor.	2.9	3.1	4.0	3.5	1.4	0.7	0.0	6.1
Unfavor.	23.7	16.2	3.4	5.5	3.4	0.7	34.4	6.1
Number of items	(796)	(579)	(350)	(860)	(442)	(149)	(163)	(98)

Several interesting findings emerge from this table. We already knew that there were far more items about Turner than about Mulroney. We now see that a higher proportion were likely to leave the reader with an unfavorable impression than was the case with Mulroney. The same is true when we compare Liberals other than Turner with Conservatives other than Mulroney. And when we compare the two parties, the difference is striking: there were more stories about the Liberal party, 34 per cent were unfavorable and not one was favorable. The Conservative party, on the other hand, received as much favorable as unfavorable coverage.

It is revealing also to examine the display given to items likely to leave an unfavorable impression on the reader. There were, for example, 203 of these items receiving a high attention score: 31.5 per cent were about Turner, 15.3 per cent about Mulroney; 10.8 per cent about the Liberal party, 1.5 per cent about the Conservative party. When we look at the 46 high attention items likely to leave a favorable impression, Turner and Mulroney each received 17.4 per cent, but 6.5 per cent were about the Conservative party and none were about the Liberal party. In other words, there were not only more items likely to create unfavorable impressions of Turner and the Liberal party than there were of Mulroney and the Conservative party, but they were more prominently displayed in the papers.

Did this pattern of favorable and unfavorable coverage run through all seven papers, or did it depend to some extent on the editorial position of the paper? Analysis reveals even-handed coverage of the leaders by the Halifax Chronicla-Herald — but that is due in large measure to the fact that the paper published mostly neutral news and little by the way of commentary and opinion. Diligent readers of each of the other six papers would probably have finished the campaign with significantly more unfavorable impressions of Turner than of Mulroney. And when it came to the two major parties, there was simply no contest: in each of the papers the Liberal party received far more unfavorable coverage than the Conservative party.

CONCLUSION

In general, the seven papers emerge well from this analysis of their election coverage. They provided ample space: on average, about 15,000 column inches each, which translates by the rule of the roughest thumb to about half-a-million words, plus headlines and illustrations. About 80 per cent of the space was devoted to news reporting, background to the news, and pictures, and the remainder to comment and opinion. They covered both national and local campaigns. The coverage was reasonably balanced as between the three national leaders and their parties. Among the policy issues debated by the candidates, they focused strongly on the state of the economy and related topics, but that seemed to reflect the interests of the voters. There was, however, a heavy concentration on the process of politics, perhaps to the exclusion of longer and better coverage of issues: the Liberal party organization and campaign became a major story that preoccupied many journalists and consumed great amounts of space and display. The same criticism might be made of the use of data from opinion polls.

In the items of coverage that could be read as directly critical of the two major party leaders — mainly opinions expressed in editorials and columns — the balance was not unreasonable in any of the papers. And taking all seven together, the two men were treated equally. But this was not true of the two major parties: the Liberal party was directly criticized far more than was the Conservative party, and this was true for all papers in the survey, suggesting that they were reflecting a nationally-held view of the situation rather than a regional or editorial bias. Apart from direct criticism, there is indirect criticism — that is to say, items that leave the reader with an unfavorable impression of the leader or party featured in the item. Here Turner suffered significantly more than Mulroney, and the Liberal party much, much more than the Conservative party.

In summary, there is no doubt that careful readers of each of the seven papers would have finished the campaign with impressions less favorable of Turner and the Liberal party than of Mulroney and the Conservative party. But there is no evidence to suggest that these impressions were the result of biased reporting or of unreasonable and unfair comment and opinion.

The appropriate question in the end may not be Who Shot J.T.?, but Who Shot the Liberal Party? The best answer is that the party shot itself, with some help from journalists who were extraordinarily interested in its problems with patronage, organization, and campaign difficulties.

TELEVISION COVERAGE

As mentioned above, while newspapers can provide comprehensive coverage of an election, many Canadians rely on television for the daily highlights of the campaign. It is probably fair to say that the major national newscasts are roughly equivalent to the front pages of the papers, so the following brief study of CBC and CTV election coverage in the major nightly newscasts is not comparable with the study of all contents of the papers. It does, however, enable us to see if there were major differences in the news judgements and priorities of the two media.

TABLE 20
Area of Coverage by Network
(Percentages)

	CBC	CTV
Issues	46.5	34.3
Process	19.5	19.8
Other	34.0	45.9
Number of items	(231)	(236)

This reverses the pattern found in the newspapers. However, it must be remembered that the more extensive newspaper coverage included commentary and opinion and other background items that would be unsuitable for a TV newscast. But it is interesting to note that the major issue for both networks was the economy, as it was for the newspapers. For the CBC, the next most important issue was national unity; for CTV it was patronage.

Two of the most important items of coverage on the newscasts were the TV debates among the party leaders and public opinion polls. These were the major topics of 22 per cent of CTV items and 14 per cent of CBC items. In fact, poll findings were mentioned in 24 per cent of CTV and 19 per cent of CBC reports.

TABLE 21
Party Mentioned in Item, by Network
(Percentages)

	CBC	CTV
Liberal party	31.2	33.9
Cons. party	24.2	22.0
NDP	19.5	17.8
All three pys.	16.0	15.7
Other or no py.	9.1	10.6
Number of items	(231)	(236)

TABLE 22
Leader Mentioned in Item, by Network
(Percentages)

	CBC	CTV
Turner	22.1	23.7
Mulroney	22.9	20.8
Broadbent	19.9	17.4
Other or no leader	35.1	38.1
Number of items	(231)	(236)

These two tables reveal a similarity in coverage by the two networks that is striking.

In summary, each network provided an average of four election items every night in its major newscast. In terms of issues, their focus was much the same as that of the newspapers — but that may mean only that journalists from the two media perceived the news in the same way, rather than that one group set the agenda for the other. In terms of the attention they paid to the leaders and the parties, their coverage was balanced, and there was virtually no difference between the two networks.

ENDNOTE

(1) Items were coded for Attention Score according to the following formula: 1 point for a headline more than two columns in width; 1 point if the headline was more than half the width of the page; 1 point if the headline was above the fold of the page; 1 point if the text, headline and accompanying picture occupied more than three-quarters of a column; one point if the item was on page one, the editorial page, or the front page of a section of the paper. An item therefore could be scored from 0 to 5 points, but for ease of analysis, the six categories were collapsed into three — Low, Medium, High.

CHAPTER 4

THE POLLS

In a steamy civic centre in Ottawa on a Friday evening in June 1984, a battle raged. It was a feud between the forces of Jean Chretien and John Turner, one of whom would be chosen Liberal leader and prime minister the next day, and the ammunition was polling data. The Chretien camp had released poll results from the Martin Goldfarb organization showing that their candidate was the one most Canadians wanted to see succeed Pierre Trudeau as prime minister. By way of reply the Turner campaign released a report from their pollster Angus Reid, showing that Turner was the candidate most likely to win a general election.

Thus at the beginning of a path that would lead to the general election, the polls were playing a role, and this role would become more and more important as the election was called and the campaign progressed. In the general election of 1984 there were more polls conducted by the media and political parties than ever before, so much so that they became an election issue in themselves.

The media use polls in covering elections to augment news reports, while parties employ them to define campaign strategies. This situation is not going to change since the polls are so important to both groups they would feel naked without them. Nevertheless, the polls were criticized throughout the election as being inaccurate, an undue influence on voting decisions and a diversion from the real issues of the election campaign. In fact media polling in Canada is modest in comparison with other Western countries. In the United States most major news organizations have in-house polling services which produce, during the extended period of primary and presidential contests, a plethora of data. They spend sums of money on this activity that would make their Canadian counterparts blush. Similarly politicians in the U.S. spend staggering amounts on polls. Though in-house polls are rare in the British media, news organizations there sponsored 47 polls in the 30 days prior to the last general election vote in 1984. (1) In Canada during the election period of 58 days there were only 12

75

national opinion polls published by the media. Despite the relative modesty of the Canadian performance the polls were widely reported and this, no doubt, raised questions about their influence on political activity.

In order to evaluate the quality and usefulness of polls in Canada it is necessary to look at how the polls are done, their accuracy, the use made of them, the criticisms of them, and what they contribute to an understanding of the 1984 election.

METHODOLOGY

Pollsters seek to discover the opinions of a large group of people — say, for example, the population of Canada — by interviewing a small sample of that group. There is no great mystery to the technique: the pollster must simply be sure that the sample is truly representative of the group in terms of age, sex, geographical location and other factors. Hard as it may be to believe, a representative sample will reflect the opinions of the whole within prescribed margins of error. Thus the core of all polling is the selection of the sample, but the method of selecting a sample may vary from pollster to pollster. It will depend on how the sample will be interviewed, the nature of the questions to be asked, and the nature of the group under study. All pollsters would agree that in an ideal world the best way of obtaining a sample would be by random selection. All this means is that each person in the population to be studied would have an equal chance of becoming a member of the sample.

But there are practical difficulties. For example, to select a sample of all Canadian voters, one would need a list of the entire adult population eligible to vote, and such a list does not exist until enumeration has been completed across the country. Furthermore, if one wanted to interview those selected in their homes, it would be impracticable to reach many of them, especially in remote areas, without almost as many interviewers as respondents. Some pollsters solve this problem by selecting population areas or clusters that collectively reflect the demographic characteristics of the population. Random sampling can then take place within these areas or clusters. The best known polling firm, the Canadian Institute of Public Opinion, better known as Gallup, uses this approach. In addition, Gallup uses quota sampling: this means that interviewers are instructed to find respondents in the areas or clusters who fit within certain age, gender and economic categories. The resulting sample should constitute a demographic profile of the population.

An alternative method of interviewing is to use the telephone instead of visiting the sample in their homes. This technique is used by an increasing number of pollsters because it permits selection of a truly national random sample, either from telephone directories or by "Random Digit Dialling" — the use of computers to randomly generate numbers from the list of all telephone exchanges. When directories are used, the problem of unlisted or out-of-date numbers is avoided by adding one or two to the last digit of the number chosen. A further technique of selection ensures that when an interviewer calls a number in the sample, each member of that household has an equal chance of being interviewed. Again, the object is to ensure that those interviewed are demographically representative of the population.

The advantage of telephone interviewing is that it has a fast "turnaround" time (the time between the completion of the interviews and the computation of the results). Also, a more random national sample can be selected and the interviewing can be conducted from a centralized, supervised location. The advantage of the "in-home" method is that there tends to be a much higher response rate. Usually about 20 per cent of those contacted by telephone are unwilling to participate.

Questionnaires are invariably pre-tested to discover whether or not there is vagueness or ambiguity in the questions or if there are areas of interest that are not being specifically investigated. In an election questionnaire there can be 30 or 40 questions dealing with issues, the vote, attitudes toward the leaders and general political orientation. Though voters are most familiar with the standard voting question, "if an election were held tomorrow, which party would you vote for", many pollsters probe much more deeply into voting intentions. They may, for example, wish to discover past voting behavior, whether the respondent intends to vote and if not, why not. Of those who intend to vote, the strength of their commitment or the reasons for their voting choice may be subjects of inquiry. Questionnaires also include standard demographic items such as age, sex, education, language and religion. These questions are not only useful for analysis, they tell the pollster how good his sample is since, with random sampling, these demographic results should reflect the population statistics.

ACCURACY

Pollsters often argue that public opinion surveys are blunt instruments of prediction. Polls are, they say, mere snapshots of opinion at a specific time and are no guarantee that opinion will not change. While this is undoubtedly true, it is an argument that appears self-serving since it can be used to justify the claim that pollsters are never wrong. No matter what the pollsters say, however, those who read the polls will evaluate their accuracy on the basis of actual voting outcomes. In this regard polls can be wrong, sometimes spectacularly so.

The largest survey ever conducted belongs in this category. In 1936 when polling was in its infancy, a U.S. magazine, *The Literary Digest* with a sample of 10,000,000, disastrously concluded Franklin Delano Roosevelt would be defeated in the presidential election of that year. The reasons for the debacle were that the sample was contacted by telephone or mail. In those days telephone ownership was restricted to the reasonably affluent, who tended to be Republican, and the Digest's mail response was only 20 per cent, resulting in a biased sample.

When polls are wrong in such an obvious way the reasons are usually methodological. It is more common for errors to be evident in close elections. In the Dewey-Truman election of 1948 the polls predicted a Dewey victory, but research after the election showed that there was a late swing to the incumbent president during the last week of the campaign in an already close race. Since there was a lag time between the interviewing and the publication of the results, the polls missed this late Truman surge. The same thing happened in the 1970 British general election. The only poll to predict a Conservative victory was the one taken closest to election day. Indeed one study after the event discovered that for all the polls, there was a direct correlation between the closeness to voting day and the accuracy of the results. (2) Thus in close elections polls can get the winner wrong even though their results are fairly close to the actual outcome and well within their margins of error. Pollsters, though, would contend that this is not getting a result wrong; it is rather a misinterpretation of survey data.

In Canada polling has a record of accuracy. The Gallup organization has been polling in federal general elections since 1945 and its record is enviable.

TABLE 1
Difference between Gallup Results and
Voting Outcomes 1945-1984*
(Percentges)

	Lib	PC	NDP	other
1945	−2	+2	+1	−1
1949	−2	+1	+2	−1
1953	+1	0	0	−1
1957	+7	−5	−1	−1
1958	0	+2	−2	0
1962	−1	+1	−2	0
1963	−1	−1	+1	+1
1965	+4	−3	0	−1
1968	+2	−2	+1	−1
1972	0	−2	+3	−1
1974	0	0	0	0
1979	−2.5	+1.5	+1	0
1980	+4	−5	+3	−1
1984	0	0	0	0

* Sources: CIPO releases
   L. Leduc, 'The Measurement of Public Opinion' in H.R. Penniman (ed.), *Canada at the Polls*, American Enterprise Institute for Public Policy Research, Washington, D.C., 1975, p. 217.

There are two problems in Canada which may limit the accuracy, or apparent accuracy, of opinion polls. The first is the political geography of Canada. Canada's size and scattered rural population make interviewing difficult. Another important aspect of this problem is the regional component in Canadian political life. Different regional interests and attitudes mean that voting patterns vary from region to region and there may be no consistent voting swing — that is, change in the vote from one party to another — across the country. In such circumstances it is virtually impossible to translate voting intentions into seats, or potential seats, in the House of Commons. In landslide elections, such as 1984, this problem is minimized since regional swings tend to be in the same direction even if they are not of the same magnitude. However, such a luxury is rare in Canadian elections. The second problem deals with the volatile nature of the Canadian electorate. After the 1980 election the Liberals held a comfortable lead in the polls. By the end of 1983 the Conservatives had a lead of around 30 percentage points, a margin unprecedented in polling history. During the first part of 1984 the Liberals enjoyed a recovery and some polls suggested they led the opposition by as much as 10 percentage points in the middle of the year.

TABLE 2
Gallup Poll Results 1980-1984*
(Percentages)

	Liberal	PC	NDP	others
February 1980	44	32	20	03
March	47	28	22	02
April	49	28	20	03
May	44	31	22	03
June	47	31	20	03
July	48	30	21	01
August	48	29	21	02
September	50	29	19	02
October	48	30	20	02
November	45	31	22	02
December	44	34	20	02
January 1981	40	34	23	03
February	42	37	19	02
March	46	35	18	02
April	43	37	19	01
May	42	37	18	02
June	43	36	19	02
July	44	37	18	02
August	42	39	16	03
September	38	39	20	03
October	40	40	18	02
November	38	42	18	02
December	35	39	22	04
January 1982	38	40	20	02
February	35	36	26	03
March	31	42	24	03
April	34	39	24	03
May	33	44	21	03
June	32	43	23	01
July	28	47	23	02
August	31	44	23	02
September	30	45	22	03
October	30	46	21	03
November	32	46	20	02
December	31	46	21	02
January 1983	31	49	20	01
February	34	45	19	01
March	30	50	17	02
April	27	52	19	02
May	32	50	16	02
June	34	50	15	02
July	27	55	16	02
August	28	50	20	02
September i)	23	62	14	01
September ii)	26	55	16	02
October	27	56	16	02

Table 2 (continued)

Gallup Poll Results 1980-1984*
(Percentages)

	Liberal	PC	NDP	others
November	—	—	—	—
December	30	53	15	02
January 1984	32	52	15	02
February	36	48	13	02
March	32	54	11	02
April	46	40	13	02
May i)	46	40	11	03
May ii)	46	42	11	01
June	49	38	11	01
July	48	39	11	02
August i)	32	46	18	04
August ii)	28	50	19	03

* Source: CIPO Releases
Note: Numbers may not add to 100 due to rounding

When opinion is volatile, polls are always trying to catch up, and any single result may be misleading. It is, then, the analysis of poll results over time that is most useful for understanding trends in public opinion. As the 1984 campaign progressed, volatility was not a problem because the trend to the Conservatives was strong and obvious. However, it may well be a problem for pollsters in future Canadian elections.

Another problem in interpreting polling results is the so-called "undecided" vote, which in the election ranged up to a high of 38 per cent. When the "undecided" vote fluctuates it is difficult to estimate what is going on and where switches in preference are taking place. This problem is compounded by the fact that different pollsters mean different things when they report "undecided" voters. Some polling firms include in the "undecided" category those who say they will not vote, those who are unsure whether they will vote, and those who will vote but are undecided as to how they will vote. Others eliminate those who say they will not vote. These differences make comparison of the polls difficult. It is even more confusing when the same pollster changes methodology. The collapse of the "undecided" vote in the Gallup polls close to the election day has in the past been shown to be a result of methodological change rather than a change in opinion.(3)

Another problem for the public in interpreting poll results is the "margin of error". This is essentially a statistical concept used by pollsters to qualify their results. Typically, a national election poll based on a sample of 1,060 would be said to be accurate "within four percentage points 19 times out of 20". This is merely an estimate that if the poll were repeated over and over again, the results would be the same within a range of 4 percentage points almost all of the time. It does not mean that the results are as likely to be out by 4 points as to be correct. Nor does it mean that the 20th poll will be wildly wrong. However, the margin of error does not include mistakes in interviewing or calculation which could also distort results. In general, the larger the sample, the smaller the margin of error.

One implication of this is that when a national sample is broken down, say by region, the sample size in each region may be small and the margin of error high. To reduce this error as much as possible, pollsters conducting a national survey may do more interviews in less populated regions in order to ensure an adequate regional sample. The effect of this "oversampling" is of course removed when national totals are reported. Despite these problems and differences, most polls agree most of the time about the state of public opinion.

POLLS AND THE MEDIA

In a sense polling is little more than an extension of normal reporting. During an election campaign a reporter follows a party leader or candidate, asks a few questions of those involved in the event being covered, confers with his fellow reporters and comes to a conclusion about the significance of the event. Pollsters simply ask questions of a more representative sample of individuals who usually will be voters and not politicians. Though journalists will continue to cover elections in the traditional way, their conclusions are becoming more and more influenced by poll results, and indeed polls are becoming major news items in themselves.

Though newspapers in the U.S. have used polling techniques since the 1820s, in Canada national polls during elections have been a phenomenon only since 1945. The media since then have become more and more enamoured with polls and their reasons are straightforward . First, polling data are reliable in explaining the development of the campaign and who is winning and who is losing. Second, such data helps the media decide what to cover; it explains the issue agenda, opinions on leaders, and the geographical areas of interest. Last, but not least, is the question of self-reliance. Without public polls news organizations would be dependent on leaks from private party polls — and such leaks are notoriously selective and biased. Though no Canadian media organization conducts its own "in-house" polls, five major news groups sponsored national polls during the 1984 election. Both national TV networks hired Toronto-based polling firms to conduct national surveys. The Globe and Mail newspaper used its regular polling firm C.R.O.P. (Centre de Rescherche sur l'Opinion Public) to produce two polls during the campaign. Southam News commissioned three national polls from the Carleton Journalism Poll of Carleton University, and Sorecom of Montreal conducted one national poll and regional polling for Le Soleil, a Quebec city daily. While most of these were exclusive and comprehensive polls, other newspapers received data from Gallup. There are essentially two forms of sponsorship. A newspaper or TV network can commission a poll. This may ask up to 30 or 40 questions. The other method is to add on questions to regular commercial surveys. These omnibus surveys are market research ventures which include some political questions. No matter what system is used, news organizations tend to get a good financial deal from pollsters who are quite willing to make only a marginal profit to obtain the publicity generated by the publication of the poll results.

In the past news organizations have tried to do "in-house" polls. During the 1974 campaign, the Globe and Mail hired an expert who advised them on polling methods. Reporters were used as interviewers and the result, according to the paper's managing editor at the time, was a disaster (4); sports reporters, sub-editors, and political writers were late with copy because of their daily quota of interviews, thus disrupting the production of the paper. TV networks have sometimes used reporters to conduct polls of delegates at political conventions.

In the 1984 election, the major news organizations hired pollsters to do their sampling, interviewing and analysis throughout the campaign. What these poll results described was a close race at the beginning of the campaign which became a Conservative triumph. In the case of Gallup and CTV, voting intentions and basic attitudes on issues and leaders were the main components of the surveys. CBC, Southam/Carleton and Globe/C.R.O.P. provided much more detailed information. The CBC poll was the basis for a one-hour TV news special, while each Globe/C.R.O.P. and Southam/Carleton poll was reported in five or six articles on specific survey topics. These newspapers polls were accompanied by articles on the methodology of the polls.

TABLE 3
1984 Election Polls: Voting Intentions

Interviewing Dates	Sample Size	PC (%)	Lib (%)	NDP (%)	Other or Won't Say	Undecided (%)
Globe-CROP						
June 18-July 8	1950	39	49	11	—	(19)
Gallup						
July 5-7	1049	39	48	11	—	(38)
Southam/Carleton						
July 4-12	1502	43	45	9	3	(32)
CTV						
July 25-31	2000	45	36	17	2	(35)
Southam/Carleton						
Aug. 1-7	1969	51	32	15.5	1.5	(31)
CBC						
Aug. 4-12	2661	49	32	18	—	(19)
Gallup						
Aug. 11-13	1033	46	32	18	2	(11)
Globe-CROP						
Aug. 14-19	1398	49	32	18	1	(17)
Southam/Carleton						
Aug. 19-22	1533	56.5	27	15	1.5	(28)
Sorecom						
Aug. 16-26	1206	50	27	21	2	(28)
CTV						
Aug. 27-29	2000	51	26	21	2	(38)
Gallup						
Aug. 28-29	2078	50	28	19	3	(10)
VOTE						
Sept. 4		49.9	28.2	18.7	3.2	

The quality, detail and methodological purity of a poll matters little if the poll is reported badly. Many of the severest critics of the way the media use polls are journalists themselves. Their criticisms fall into three categories.

1) Sponsors of polls tend to report the results at such length and with such display that they neglect other important election items.
2) The media report only the "horse race" aspect of polls rather than offer serious analysis of trends and opinions.
3) News organizations report results without reference to methodology or qualifications, such as error margins.

In order to evaluate these criticisms an analysis was conducted of all articles mentioning polls in the seven newspapers surveyed throughout the election campaign. (5)

TABLE 4
Poll Items as a Percentage of Total Election Coverage
(Percentages)

	V.Sun	W.FP	T.Star	M.Gaz	M.LP	H.C-H	G & M
Items mentioning polls	12.1	10.2	14.4	14.4	10.9	6.0	9.6
Other election coverage	87.9	89.8	85.6	85.6	90.1	94.0	90.4
Number of items	(739)	(768)	(1035)	(581)	(1043)	(631)	(813)

The papers sponsoring their own polls were The Globe and Mail, the Vancouver Sun and the Montreal Gazette. The lowest concentrations of poll stories was found in the Halifax Chronicle-Herald, the Winnipeg Free Press and The Globe and Mail — two papers not sponsoring polls and one that did. So in terms of overall coverage there does not appear to be a consistent pattern of poll-overkill by poll sponsors.

When poll articles were analysed for content many were found to mention polls in a general context. But of those that presented actual findings, 63 per cent dealt with the election as a horse race. This does not mean that this was the only topic of the item, but only that it was a prominent part.

Although newspapers are encouraged to describe the methodology of polls when reporting the findings, many do not. The Canadian Daily Newspaper Publishers Association (CDNP) has advised newspapers that when reporting survey data they should outline the sample size, the sample selection procedures, the dates the interviews were conducted, the actual questions asked and the error estimates. Clearly, if general poll findings are mentioned in a secondary way in columns, editorials or news backgrounders, such stipulations do not apply. When the primary election poll articles that reported specific findings were analysed it was found that it was not likely that methodology would be explained, and this was true of all newspapers in the sample.

What these results show is that if newspapers report polls badly, then they all do so in roughly the same way, and that sponsorship is not a significant factor. It does appear, however, that newspapers are more likely to report on methodology than in the past. Almost a quarter of all poll stories mentioned methodology.

Polling data are not only reported as news, but become the basis for much other election coverage and commentary.

TABLE 5
Type of Coverage using Polling Data
(Percentages)

News	57.1
News backgrounder	27.8
Editorial	4.1
Column	9.5
Cartoon/Photo	1.5
Number of items	(630)

Newspapers and TV networks pay substantial amounts of money for polling services. The largest and most detailed election poll in 1984 was done for the CBC. Though the CBC did most of the computer analysis in its own Toronto research unit, the corporation paid in the region of $65,000 for the basic polling service. For three national election polls, Southam News paid $50,000. But these sums are tiny compared to what the political parties pay for polling.

PARTY POLLS

When polling, political parties are much less concerned than the media with the horse-race aspect of an election. They are more interested in general public attitudes and specific opinions on issues, parties, and leaders. The parties use this data to plan and monitor their campaigns, and this is assisted by the use of frequent tracking polls to detect changes in public opinion.

Both the Conservatives and the Liberals tracked throughout the campaign. The Liberals conducted surveys of 700 respondents selected randomly throughout the country; during the middle of the campaign these polls were conducted every second night. In total the Liberals surveyed 25,000 Canadians. The Conservatives did nightly tracking with samples of 450 respondents chosen from constituencies regarded as strategic, and compiled the results into three-night averages. In addition, major national polls were used by all the parties to develop overall strategy. The parties are reluctant to say exactly how much they spent on polling but some information is available. The Liberal tracking polls cost them $330,000, and a national poll conducted prior to the election call cost them in the region of $250,000. Given that other private polling was done for them, it is unlikely their polling bill was less that $750,000. Estimates of the Conservatives' bill are in the region of $800,000. The NDP concede that their expenses were much more modest: less than $250,000 would not be surprising.

Some politicians suspect that pollsters are a dangerous new breed of political advisors, emphasizing numbers rather than issues and usurping the consulting role of regional leaders and backbenchers. While there may be an element of truth in this, the reason why they are used is that they provide more reliable and useful information than traditional sources. In the 1984 election there were, on the other hand, quite severe limitations on the "guru" role ascribed to pollsters. The NDP organizers have never believed strongly in the power of pollsters and tend to develop their own conclusions from polling data. In the case of the

Tories, the appointment of Decima Research as their polling organization was delayed because Decima's Allan Gregg had been associated with the former party leader Joe Clark. Though Gregg did eventually do the polling for the Conservatives, the Mulroney team included individuals who were comfortable with statistical analysis. The Liberal campaign was characterized by internecine feuding, and this included an intense battle for supremacy between Angus Reid and Martin Goldfarb, both of them Liberal pollsters, with Reid conducting the tracking polls, and Goldfarb the national and Ontario polls. If these factors limited the influence of political pollsters, they were hardly political eunuchs. Since polling, unlike advertising, is not restricted by the election expenses act, polling budgets are large and will, in the future, get larger. This in itself confers influence. The expenditure of the national parties was considerable, but there were also individual riding polls. Though it is impossible to determine the total figure spent by politicians on polls during the election, it far overshadows the figure spent by the media.

CRITICISMS

In general the attitude of a politician towards opinion polls is highly correlated with his/her standing in them. In the 1984 election, however, criticism came from individuals in both major parties. Liberal campaign manager Keith Davey accused the polls of destroying party morale by understating Liberal support. Geills Turner, wife of Liberal leader John Turner, suggested that news organizations that conducted polls were biased in favour of the Conservatives. The attack on the media as biased was strange; the media used independent pollsters, and if those analyses were biased they were remarkably unanimous in their bias.

More serious criticisms were raised by then External Affairs Minister Chretien and Tory Sinclair Stevens, both of whom urged a ban on the publication of poll results during federal election campaigns. This argument was based on the view that the polls influenced voting patterns and that poll results deflected interest from the issues in the election. The academic literature on the topic of influence on voting does not lend credence to the critics' argument. Though political scientists have established detailed models of voting choice, at no time has public opinion polling been seen to be a factor. Partisanship, age, sex, region and language have all been, at one time or another, important correlates with the vote in Canada, but polls have not been shown to be influential. People tend to vote for substantial reasons. Nevertheless, some politicians and pundits cite the "bandwagon" or "underdog" effects as being potential ways in which polls can influence the vote. This assumes that voters are aware of poll results, believe them to be true, and base a choice on them. The evidence of the 1984 election suggests that this is not so, in that pollsters were consistently catching up with public opinion rather than forming it, and their findings were as surprising to them as they were to others involved in the campaign. This was particularly true in the case of Quebec. There have been suggestions that Quebeckers, sensing the change of political direction in the rest of the country, decided to join the trend. The evidence is, however, to the contrary. The polls indicate that the switch to the Conservatives in Quebec happened before there was evidence of a landslide elsewhere and that from fairly early on in the race, attitude changes in Quebec continued in step with the rest of the country.

One example that is more difficult to understand is the case of Vancouver Quadra. Three polls taken in the riding fairly early in the campaign showed John Turner trailing his Conservative opponent. In fact, Turner won the seat and some commentators have suggested that voters may have interpreted poll results to mean that they could have the best of all worlds; a Conservative government and a sitting member who was also the Leader of the Liberal Opposition. Whether it was this or a "sympathy factor" is unclear. It should be remembered, though, that the Liberals recognised the danger of a loss in Quadra and mounted a considerable campaign effort as election day drew closer.

Whether one accepts the criticisms of the pollls or not, a ban on the publication of poll results would give politicians a considerable advantage over the voters. They would have information derived from their private polls; the public would be left in the dark.

POLLS AND VOTE

Polls help us to understand what happened in the election by showing how public opinion developed in the years before the election and then during the campaign itself. As Table 2 shows, the Conservatives enjoyed a commanding lead over the Liberals from May 1982, reaching a peak in September, 1983, and hovering around 30 percentage points for several months. Even as late as Gallup's March, 1984, report, the Conservatives still had a 22 point lead. Then with Prime Minister Trudeau's decision to resign, the emergence of John Turner as a candidate to succeed him, and the focus on the Liberal leadership race, there was a sudden turnaround. For a few months, the Liberals took a narrow lead, but party and media polls showed that support for the Liberals was soft — that is, not firmly committed and liable to switch to another party. This was confirmed when the campaign began and Liberal support quickly evaporated. By election day, the Conservatives again had a 22 point lead, reverting to the position of half a year earlier. What this suggests is that while at one point the Liberals had a chance to win the election, it was never a strong one. The voters wavered only briefly in their longstanding intentions to defeat the Liberals and elect the Conservatives. During the campaign, the Liberals were more vulnerable than the other parties, and Turner's blunders and failures merely reactivated the underlying desire for change.

The decline of the Liberals and the rise of the Conservatives during the campaign was shown clearly by the polls. The most remarkable change of course was in Quebec, and without the evidence of the polls the extent of this shift in party support would not have been fully understood or reported. The polls were also able to measure the impact of specific campaign events, such as the TV debates. The evidence seems to show that Conservative support peaked about two weeks before voting day. The party's own tracking polls showed a slight erosion after that point, and the NDP appear to have been the beneficiaries.

ENDNOTES

(1) D. Butler, D. Kavanagh, *The British General Election of 1983*, London, Macmillan, 1984, p. 125
(2) R. Rose (ed.), *The Polls and the 1970 Election*, Survey Research Centre, Occasional Paper No. 7, University of Strathclyde, Glasgow, 1970
(3) This was stated by a representative of CIPO at a meeting of the Canadian Association for Applied Statistical Research in Saskatoon, June, 1979
(4) Clark Davey, in a speech to the Couchiching Institute on Public Affairs, University of Toronto, February, 1985
(5) See Chapter 3

CHAPTER 5

ANALYSIS OF THE VOTE

There are a number of ways in which to analyse patterns of voting in an election. We can look at how the vote was distributed by province, and at how it was distributed by sex, language and other factors. In addition, we can examine the level of participation, and see how accurately the number of MPs elected for each party .reflected the popular vote. All this should lead us to a better understanding of the nature of the support for each of the parties and of the underlying significance of the election.

GEOGRAPHY OF THE VOTE

The most striking feature of the vote in recent Canadian general elections has been the regional distribution. Prior to the election of 1984, the West was strongly Conservative, Quebec was dominated by the Liberals, and the remainder of the country was a battleground in each election. So much was this the case that it was conventional political wisdom that elections were won and lost in Ontario where 95 seats were up for grabs. The fact that the Liberals elected few members in the West and the Conservatives were more or less shut-out in Quebec led to demands for a new electoral system based on proportional representation — that is to say, a system that would more accurately relate the number of seats won by each party to the votes it obtained. A crucial fact about the 1984 election is that the familiar pattern of voting was smashed: the Conservatives were the winning party in every province, in terms both of the popular vote and of seats won in the House of Commons, a feat not achieved even in the great Conservative landslide in 1958.

The following table summarizes the shift in votes from 1980 to 1984.

TABLE 1
Votes by Party for Each Province, 1980 and 1984
(Percentages)

| | 1980 | | | | 1984 | | | |
	PC	Lib	NDP	Others	PC	Lib	NDP	Others
Nfld.	36	47	17	—	58	36	6	—
PEI	46	47	7	—	52	41	6	1
N.S.	39	40	21	—	51	34	15	—
N.B.	33	50	16	1	54	32	14	—
Que.	13	68	9	10	50	35	9	6
Ont.	36	42	22	—	48	30	21	1
Man.	38	28	34	—	43	22	27	8
Sask.	39	24	36	1	42	18	38	2
Alta.	66	21	10	3	69	12	14	5
B.C.	41	22	35	2	47	16	35	2
Y/NWT	32	37	31	—	47	25	24	4
Canada	33	44	20	3	50	28	19	3

Source: Reports of Chief Electoral Officer

The Conservatives could have won the election without Quebec, but the huge swing there turned the tide into a tidal wave, and for the first time since 1968 the country had a government with strong representation from every region.

PARTICIPATION

In many Western countries the proportion of those entitled to vote in national elections who do vote, has been falling. For example, in the last Presidential election in the United States, only slightly more than half the electorate chose to cast their ballots, raising questions about the mandate of the Reagan Administration. In Canada, some commentators suggested there might be a similar alienation from politics, and this could have been exacerbated when it became apparent during the 1984 campaign that a Conservative victory was a foregone conclusion: why vote if the decision has already been made? In fact, the turnout went from 69 per cent in 1980 to 75 per cent in 1984. This was not,

TABLE 2
Turnout in Federal Elections
(Percentages)

1930	74	1963	79
1935	74	1965	75
1940	70	1968	76
1945	75	1972	77
1949	74	1974	71
1953	68	1979	76
1957	74	1980	69
1958	79	1984	75
1962	79		

Source: Reports of Chief Electoral Officer

however, an unusual rush of voters to the polls: since the system of house-to-house enumeration when an election is called was introduced in 1930, the rate of turnout has remained remarkably stable.

Not only was the level of national turnout about average, but turnout in each of the provinces was consistent with long term patterns.

TABLE 3
Turnout by Province in 1985

Nfld.	65%
P.E.I.	85%
N.S.	75%
N.B.	77%
Que.	76%
Ont.	76%
Man.	73%
Sask.	78%
Alta.	69%
B.C.	78%
Yukon	78%
NWT	68%

Source: Reports of the Chief Electoral Officer

In the majority of elections since 1945 Prince Edward Island has had the highest rate of turnout. Since joining Confederation, Newfoundland has usually had the lowest rate. Of the Western provinces, Saskatchewan has generally had the highest rate. Thus the Conservative victory in 1984 was not the result of heavy voting in areas of Conservative strength or of low voting in areas of traditional Liberal strength.

DISPROPORTIONAL REPRESENTATION

The fact that the election produced a government with strong support in all regions of the country does not mean that it reflected the wishes of the people as expressed in the vote. Various types of proportional representation have been discussed by academics and politicians, but if the popular vote for each party in 1984 were to be accurately translated into seats, the composition of the House of Commons would be much different.

TABLE 4
Seats in the Commons

	1984 Election	Under PR
Conservatives	211	142
Liberals	40	79
NDP	30	53
Other	1	8

Thus under PR in its purest form the Conservatives would still have had a majority in the Commons — but of only two seats. Even if PR had been based on the vote in each province, rather than on the national vote as in the table above, the result would still have been a Conservative majority of two seats: Conservatives, 142; Liberals, 81; NDP, 52; Others, 7.

MARGINALS

That the Conservatives would have won a majority of seats even under the PR is one measure of the scale of their victory. Another measure is that despite having a huge majority of seats the Conservatives hold only a few more marginal seats than the Liberals. A marginal seat is defined here as a riding where the margin of victory of the winning candidate over his closest opponent is less than five per cent. Of the 43 seats in this category, where a small swing in votes could result in a gain or loss for a party, the Conservatives hold 17 while the Liberals hold 14. Though the Liberals have only 40 seats in the House of Commons 14 of them are vulnerable.

TABLE 5
Marginals

	Parties Holding Seat	Margin of Victory	Nearest Rival
Ontario (16)			
Algoma	Lib	3.6%	PC
Brant	NDP	2.7%	PC
Kenora—Rainy Valley	NDP	1.8%	PC
Oshawa	NDP	3.5%	PC
Ottawa Centre	NDP	0.1%	PC
Renfrew—Nipissing—Pembroke	Lib	0.1%	PC
Stormont—Dundas	PC	4.8%	Lib
Thunder Bay—Nipigon	NDP	3.2%	Lib
Windsor—Walkerville	NDP	2.7%	PC
York North/York-Nord	ind	4.8%	PC
Eglinton—Lawrence	Lib	2.7%	PC
Etobicoke North	PC	1.6%	Lib
Parkdale—High Park	PC	3.7%	Lib
Spadina	NDP	4.0%	Lib
Willowdale	PC	0.7%	Lib
Quebec (13)			
Hull—Aylmer	Lib	3.6%	PC
La Prairie	PC	2.0%	Lib
Saint-Hyacinthe—Bagot	PC	3.3%	Lib
Shefford	Lib	4.6%	PC
Bourassa	Lib	3.4%	PC
Hochelaga—Maisonneuve	PC	3.2%	Lib
Laval-Des-Rapides	Lib	4.6%	PC
Papineau	Lib	2.1%	PC
Rosemont	PC	3.5%	Lib
Saint-Jacques	Lib	2.1%	PC
Saint-Leonard—Anjou	Lib	2.1%	PC
Saint-Michel—Ahuntsic	Lib	4.5%	PC
Verdun—Saint-Paul	PC	2.3%	Lib

Table 5 (continued)

Marginals

	Parties Holding Seat	Margin of Victory	Nearest Rival
New Brunswick (1)			
Westmorland—Kent	Lib	3.8%	PC
Manitoba (1)			
Selkirk—Interlake	PC	2.0%	NDP
British Columbia (4)			
Comox—Powell River	NDP	1.2%	PC
Cowichan—Malahat—The Islands	NDP	3.0%	PC
Kootenay West	PC	2.2%	NDP
Nanaimo—Alberni	PC	2.9%	NDP
Saskatchewan (4)			
Mackenzie	PC	1.9%	NDP
Prince Albert	NDP	0.8%	PC
Saskatoon East	PC	0.9%	NDP
The Battlefords—Meadowlake	PC	1.1%	NDP
Newfoundland (3)			
Burin—St. George's	PC	1.1%	Lib
Grand Falls—White Bay— Labrador	Lib	2.8%	PC
Humber—Port Au Port — St. Barbe	Lib	1.4%	PC
Northwest Territories (1)			
Nunatsiaq	PC	3.6%	Lib

WHO VOTED FOR WHOM

Voting statistics tell us who won and lost. To discover the types of voters who make up these statistics we can examine opinion polls taken during the election campaign. But it must be kept in mind that polling data is less precise than actual voting results; votes are counted officially while polls depend on how people say they intend to vote, and on how accurately they later recall how they did vote. There is a margin of error and the figures should be read as indicating trends rather than as precise reports. The Carleton Journalism Poll conducted three national surveys for Southam News during the election campaign, the last being two weeks prior to election day. Respondents were asked not only about how they intended to vote and reasons for their intention, but were identified by sex, language used at home, and other demographic factors. This enabled pollsters to track the way in which voting intentions changed in various groups during the course of the campaign. Early in the campaign, the Liberals were leading. By mid-campaign, the Conservatives had surged ahead, taking support from the Liberals among almost all groups of voters. In the final stages, the Conservatives consolidated a coalition of voters that eliminated many of the differences that had distinguished party support at the outset. For example, there was much talk early in the election about a gender gap: women were more likely than men to support the Liberals, while men favored the Conservatives. The following table shows that this difference disappeared as the campaign progressed and women moved to the Conservatives.

TABLE 6
Vote by Gender
(Percentages of Decided Voters)

| | Poll 1 | | Poll 2 | | Poll 3 | |
	Men	Women	Men	Women	Men	Women
PC	46	39	53	49	58	54
Lib	41	50	31	34	25	30
NDP	10	8	15	15	15	14
Other	3	3	1	2	2	2

Source: Southam/Carleton Poll. Poll 1 taken July 4-12; Poll 2 taken August 1-7; Poll 3 taken August 19-22.

Analysis of the vote by language-spoken-at-home shows a similar trend: Liberal support eroding, Conservative support growing so that by the end of the campaign the Conservatives were stronger among all groups.

TABLE 7
Vote by Language Spoken at Home
(Percentages of Decided Voters)

| | Poll 1 | | | Poll 2 | | | Poll 3 | | |
	Eng	Fr	Other	Eng	Fr	Other	Eng	Fr	Other
Cons	48	27	29	54	45	37	57	57	44
Lib	39	63	60	27	42	56	25	31	34
NDP	12	3	7	18	8	6	16	7	20
Other	1	7	4	1	5	1	2	5	2

Source: Southam/Carleton Poll

Although the Conservatives in the end had a plurality among voters whose language spoken at home was other than English or French — the so-called Ethnic vote — the Liberals still did better among this group than among any other.

At the outset of the campaign, polling data indicated that the Liberals had an advantage among voters in the youngest and oldest age groups, and among those with a low level of education. The Conservatives tended to do best among the middle aged. By the end of the campaign, the Conservatives had a substantial majority in all groups. The Conservatives' winning coalition in fact was spread fairly evenly across all sections of the population. So the election may have been more than just an event that swept the Conservatives into power with a huge majority; it may have been a watershed in terms of voting patterns in Canada.

A WATERSHED ELECTION?

The traditional coalition of voters that had made the Liberals the governing party for most of this century obviously disintegrated in 1984. The question which remains is whether this was a temporary phenomenon indicating only that the voters wanted to be rid of an unpopular administration, or whether it revealed a fundamental shift in party support, making the Conservatives the new governing party. Only time will provide a decisive answer, but clues can be gained from examining the work of social scientists who have studied voting patterns in Canada and in other democracies. For example, if one could relate voting decisions to age, class, sex or other factors, one could begin to understand what motivates voters, and thus to predict how they will behave in the future. Unfortunately, it is not as simple as that. After all, the individual voter bases his or her decisions on a variety of factors, such as the issues in an election, attitudes towards leaders, sentiments in the group to which he or she belongs, and past attachments to one of the parties. To build a model of voting, it is necessary to take into account not only variables such as age, sex and religion, but also the social and psychological make-up of the voter, which leads to further complications for the theorists. But it is fair to say that in most models of voting in democracies, party identification — or in other words, the party with which a voter identifies and traditionally supports — is the most important variable in determining how the individual will vote.

Presumably association with a party depends on the ideology of the party or the interests it represents. But in Canada parties do not seem to be differentiated along these lines. There appears to be little or no difference between the major parties on a left/right dimension. (1) It is clear that such factors as region and language influence voting, but it is not clear how those influences are transmitted through partisanship. Because of this John Meisel has suggested an alternative to partisanship: Party Image. (2) He measured the degree to which the major parties deviated from an ideal party in the mind of the voter. The Liberals deviated least from those items on the scale that concerned age, competence, dullness, weakness and modernity. In other words if respondents picked an ideal position on the scale for these items, the Liberals, more than the other parties, approximated to this position. Using these findings he argued that the model of voting could be described as values and environment mediated through party image to influence vote. The difficulty with this approach is that party image is much more vague than party identification, and would be much more likely to change due to circumstance or to new party leadership.

Part of the problem is that the parties themselves may try to avoid a specific image. One study argues that the parties advocate safe, general policies, such as desire for economic advancement, in order to generate support from all quarters and alienate none. (3) They attempt to appear businesslike and promote the charms of their leader in order to avoid controversy. This has led to a weak differentiation between the parties as they all attempt to capture the middle-ground. (4) One comment on the most successful modern Canadian political party and its approach in the 1950's is still apt: "The dreading of political controversy, the silence and greyness which clothed political life in the 1950's were reflections of a Liberal ideal of an apolitical life." (5) Under this model partisanship is weak and will be less influential than other factors under most conditions. But there is an alternative theory, and that is that partisanship remains important but is changing in nature.

When Canadians are asked if they identify with one or another political party many of them are. A recent study goes further and argues that in the period 1974-80 the number who did actually increased. (6) What is surprising about this is that there was a remarkable instability in voting preferences during this period. The same study found that only 41 per cent of the electorate voted the same way in all three elections during this time, and concluded that at least in terms of voting: "A majority of the electorate have either unstable, weak or inconsistent partisan attachments." (7) It may be that while there is still a significant level of party affiliation, it is declining in strength or intensity. A decline in commitment might explain the upsurge of volatility in voting intentions evident over the last 10 years.

The debate over the importance of party affiliation may seem arcane, but it is important for an understanding of present and future Canadian politics. Those who say that party affiliation is still important could argue that the Conservative interregnum of 1957-63 backs up their claim: a weary and unpopular Liberal administration was thrown out, but when the Conservatives lost their lustre there was a national reversion to traditional affiliations which favored the Liberals. The elections of 1979 and 1980 may have been another example of this process. According to this view it would be foolish to read too much into the huge Conservative victory of 1984. If on the other hand there is a weakening in the strength of traditional partisanship, there exists a potential for new party attachments to be formed and the Liberals could be supplanted by the Conservatives as the traditional party of power.

If party identification is a less reliable indicator of voting preferences, then in the last election, the vote was influenced by other factors, such as issues and party leaders.

ISSUES

Not surprisingly during election campaigns, there is much talk about issues. Politicians are urged to "stick to the issues" and media organizations establish "issue units" or "issue teams" to cover the campaign. Voters do mention that issues are important to them in making an election choice, and the evidence suggests that the concern with issues has increased over the last few elections. (8) Surveys have discovered, however, that when respondents are asked to name the issues that are important to them they define them very broadly, such as the state of the economy or unemployment. Moreover, in many cases supporters of all the major parties agree to a remarkable degree on what the most important issues are. For an issue to influence electoral choice it must be important and must divide the political parties. Both of these provisions have, perhaps, become less evident in recent Canadian politics. One study discovered that there, "has been a propensity to shift the type of issue considered most important from one election to the next. Accompanying such shifts has been a high degree of variability in the way the same types of issues — e.g. economic, confederation — have been defined." (9) This suggests that the issues agenda is highly variable, and public willingness to accept this means that politicians or the mass media can establish the campaign agenda.

Though specific issues can be much talked about during an election, they rarely become overwhelming in the voter's mind. Surveys from the 1984 election indicate that specific topics, such as patronage, which received much media attention, are mentioned as important issues by only 2 to 3 per cent of voters. Even women's issues, the subject of a Leaders' debate, were not mentioned by more than 3 per cent of respondents. (10) This does not mean that voters had no opinions on these issues. Indeed when asked about specific issues many voters did have opinions on them. But between one quarter and one third of the electorate could not mention any important issue, and those who could often identified very general topics. This suggests that it is not specific issues which determine votes, but perhaps constellations of issues which set a mood, or a general disposition, towards a government or party.

LEADERS

Increasingly elections are being seen as contests between leaders rather than as confrontations between policy stands or ideological positions. This reflects the reality of the increasing power of leaders within their own parties and of changes in campaign strategy. In response to the question as to whether party leaders, the parties or local candidates were most important in their voting choice, 30 per cent of respondents in 1965, 42 per cent in 1968, and 33 per cent in 1974 mentioned party leaders. (11) In addition, of respondents in a 1974 survey, 25 per cent gave "party leaders" as their "real reason" — or overall reason — for voting choice. (12)

Despite the importance of the leaders' images, voters were unable to define in detail what those images were. When asked what they like or dislike about a leader, surveys show that only a minority of the electorate can be specific. (13) Generally the image of the leader is related to the popularity of the party, though the correlation is not perfect. Despite losing the 1979 federal election, the Liberal leader, Trudeau, had a higher popularity rating than his rival, Clark. Similarly there is a strong correlation between a leader's image and partisanship, though again there are exceptions to the rule. Clark as leader of the Conservatives was, at times, less popular with many Conservative supporters than Trudeau. The image of party leaders is, then, important. But since image tends to vary with party popularity, the question remains as to which influences which.

ELECTORAL CAMPAIGNS

Canadian parties are efficient contacting voters during the campaign. The major parties manage to get literature into the hands of about two-thirds of the electorate, have a canvasser contact about one-fifth, and even have their candidates talk to about one out of every 10 voters. (14) It has been estimated that about one half of the electorate have made up their mind whom to vote for by the time an election is called, and the other 50 per cent may not be entirely neutral. (15) There has been little evidence in the past that campaigns in themselves have had a direct effect on voting or that they have changed many minds. For example, though there is little chance of escape from extensive media coverage of campaigns, respondents to surveys rarely cite media accounts of the campaign as a reason for a voting decision. It may be that the real purpose of a campaign, and the real effect of media coverage, has been to reinforce existing predispositions rather than to change intentions.

However, it may be that campaigns are becoming more important in Canadian elections. In a situation where the electorate is volatile and open to persuasion, campaign strategy is likely to become much more important, but also much more risky. If a campaign can entice a potential voter into the fold, it can also alienate that voter. It is necessary, then, for the campaign to be highly structured and managed.

An example of how true this is can be found in the last election where the campaign of the Liberal party became an issue in the election. Not only did Liberal campaign blunders receive widespread exposure in the media, polling evidence throughout the election indicated that the blunders were an issue in the minds of the voters, even if a relatively minor one. A volatile electorate might also encourage negative campaigning. As making strong and clear policy statements could lose some votes, it would make sense to be fuzzy on policy, and to be direct only on areas where the opponent is known to be weak. This appears to have been the Conservative strategy in 1984.

MAKING DECISIONS

According to John Meisel, almost any statement made about Canadian voting behavior as a whole can be shown to be strongly contradicted in some region or in some section of the population. (16) However, perhaps the best way to summarize the evidence and to answer the question about whether the 1984 election marked a fundamental shift in party support is to say that while party affiliation remains an important factor in deciding how people will vote, the reasons for affiliation to a party may have changed. Instead of being based on long-term considerations such as parental influence, region, language or ethnicity, voting choice may now be determined by short-term considerations such as party image, policies and leadership. If that is so, Liberals can no longer rely on traditional party loyalty in specific regions and among particular groups. But neither can the Conservatives. As pointed out in the Preliminary Report from the 1984 National Election Study, "what the Conservative Party has gained is an opportunity to try to re-establish a sustaining national base that it has lacked since the First World War." (17)

ENDNOTES

(1) J.F. Zipp, "Left Right Dimensions of Canadian Party Identification" *Canadian Journal of Political Science*, 11, June 1978, pp. 251-277
(2) John Meisel, *Working Papers on Canadian Politics*. Montreal, McGill-Queen's University Press, 1973, p. 82
(3) Beck, Dooley, "Party Images in Canada" in H. Thorburn, (ed.), *Party Politics in Canada*. Scarborough, Prentice Hall, 1967, pp. 76-86
(4) H. Schwartz, *Public Opinion and Canadian Identity*. Berkeley, University of California Press, p. 208
(5) R. Whitaker, *The Government Party*. Toronto, University of Toronto Press, 1977, p. 420
(6) Harold Clarke et al., *Absent Mandate*. Toronto, Gage, 1984, pp. 55-75
(7) *Ibid.*, pp. 65-75
(8) *Ibid.*, p. 96
(9) *Ibid.*, p. 97
(10) Southam Carleton Polls. Published by Southam News throughout the election.
(11) Harold Clarke et al., *Political Choice in Canada*. Toronto, McGraw-Hill Ryerson, 1980, p. 135
(12) *Ibid.*
(13) Southam Carleton Polls.
(14) Clarke et al., *Political Choice*, p. 195
(15) *Ibid.*, p. 184
(16) J. Meisel (ed.), *Papers on the 1962 Election*. Toronto, University of Toronto Press, 1965, p. 286
(17) B. Kay et al., "The Character of Electoral Change: A Preliminary Report from the 1984 National Election Study". A Paper prepared for the 1985 Annual Meeting of the Canadian Political Science Association, University of Montreal, Montreal, May/June 1985.

CHAPTER 6

CONCLUSIONS

The end of the Second World War in 1945 brought a new era in Canada, new in politics as in every other phase of national life. It is an appropriate point therefore at which to begin a brief review of general elections to create a perspective in which to look closely at the election 1984. The Liberal party had formed the wartime government and narrowly won the election of 1945. In the years following, it won eight of twelve national elections and governed for more than 30 years. The Progressive Conservative party won four elections but enjoyed only half a dozen years of power; often, its victories produced precarious minorities unable to survive for long in office. It is not surprising therefore that Canadians came to look upon the Liberals as the all-powerful, natural governing party. The huge defeat suffered by the Liberals in 1984 seemed in that light to be a change in the natural order. But in fact the Liberals had not for years been as strong as myth and the superficial record suggested. They had been lucky to squeak through to victory in 1965 and 1972 when a few thousand votes changing a few seats would have put the Conservatives in power. Not once in the postwar elections had they won 50 per cent of the vote, but they had usually been able to rely on the split in the opposition vote between the PCs and the New Democratic Party (formerly the Co-operative Commonwealth Federation) to keep them in office. And as a trump card, they had enjoyed overwhelming support in Quebec — enough on most necessary occasions to offset their lack of success in other regions.

TABLE 1
Results by Region in 12 Elections 1949-1980 Inclusive
(Majorities / Pluralities of Seats)

	Liberal	Conservative
Atlantic	4	8
Quebec	11	1
Ontario	8	4
West	2	10

It is clear that the Liberals have not consistently been a strong national party. In fact, they have not won a majority of the seats in the West since 1953, and in recent times they have been almost wiped out west of Ontario. In the Atlantic region, they have been on balance the second party. In Ontario they have had more ups than downs, but the Conservatives have usually been strong second runners. In Quebec, Liberal victories have been overwhelming in number and in size. The point is, however, that once the Quebec fortress fell, the Liberals would be seen to be much weaker in national terms than had generally been recognized.

It was obvious by 1979 that the country was tiring of the years of Liberal government under the leadership of Prime Minister Trudeau. The Conservatives won the election of that year, taking 134 of the seats outside Quebec to only 47 for the Liberals. The following year, the Liberals recaptured power but they were still the second party outside Quebec: 73 Liberals to 102 Conservatives. The Liberal grip on government had become tenuous indeed, depending mainly on the loyalty of Quebec.

The elections of 1979 and 1980 seem to have been even more negative than usual: that is to say, on both occasions the voters were more concerned to dismiss a government than to elect another, and this contributed to the rising tide of political turmoil and public controversy. By September, 1981, the polls showed that the country had again changed its mind about which party to support: the Conservatives overtook the Liberals in the Gallup Poll, and from that time they continued to increase their popularity, even with Clark as their leader. After Mulroney replaced Clark as leader in the summer of 1983, Conservative support soared to a high of 62 per cent in September, while support for the Liberals slumped to 23 per cent. This was probably a "blip" in public opinion engendered by the publicity surrounding the Conservative leadership contest and by the emergence of Mulroney as an attractive new figure — the first Conservative leader from Quebec. But even when the "blip" subsided, the Conservatives still had a decisive lead over the Liberals. The desire for a change of government was strong. It was not so obvious at the time, but it is apparent now that by the beginning of 1984 the Liberal party was in serious straits, not at all a mighty fortress but a crumbling castle, divided within, attacked from without, sapped and mined below, and likely to be destroyed in the approaching election. But some hope still seemed to lie in changing its leader: the retirement of the unpopular Trudeau might satisfy some voters, and the choice of a suitable new figure might reassure the business community which had found the Trudeau Administration too interventionist for its taste, appeal to the alienated West, and charm the Yuppie electorate of Ontario. Loyal Quebec was not thought to be a problem. Turner was chosen as the new leader because he seemed best to fit the Liberal needs of the hour. The polls seemed at first to confirm the wisdom of this move when the long-standing Conservative lead disappeared, and the Liberals moved 10 points ahead. But now Turner was to make his first major mistake, by moving at once to call an election. What persuaded him is a matter of dispute. John Meisel, the distinguished political scientist and analyst, has since argued that the Liberals' belief that they could win despite the state of the government and the party was typical of Liberal arrogance. (1) Another view is that the caucus was more desperate than enthusiastic; it feared that the economic and political situation was likely to get worse rather than better by fall and was willing to gamble on the hope presented by the polls after the leadership convention. But that brief period of Liberal leadership in the polls proved to be no more than a "blip". With the start of the election campaign, the Liberals began to slip, while the Conservatives rose, and before the end of July the Conservatives were again in the lead and heading for victory.(2) The essential question to ask about the campaign is why this happened. Several answers are possible and need to be examined.

IDEOLOGY

Had there been in the 1980s a shift to the right in the ideological climate so that the Conservatives and not the centrist Liberal party now appealed to the majority and were the natural governing party? The success of neo-conservatives in Britain and the United States in capturing conservative parties and then winning elections leads one to look for evidence of a similar trend in Canada. And there is no doubt that right-inclined Conservatives were prominent in the movement to remove Clark from the leadership and install Mulroney who was thought to be less "Red" and more business oriented. There is also some evidence that Canadians in general had come to think of themselves as being rather more conservative in the sense of having less confidence in government and more in business enterprise. A CBC poll during the campaign found that 71 per cent of respondents agreed with the statement that there was too much government interference in the lives of Canadians — although the poll also showed that in some cases they wanted more government services. This ambiguity was reflected in the Conservative campaign which combined the rhetoric of conservatism with a promise to maintain and even improve essential public services. However, ideology has never been a powerful influence on Canadian voters, and there is little evidence that it was a major factor in 1984. Mulroney, while happy to accept the support of his right-wingers, indicated by his actions and statements that he wanted to be seen as a centrist, wholly committed to the social security system which the Liberals wanted to claim as their own. In this, he correctly read the minds of the electorate who might think of themselves as becoming more conservative but wanted no drastic cuts in public services.

IMAGES OF LEADERS

Leadership is a crucial factor in elections, and it may be that the voters turned against the Liberals in 1984 simply because Turner appeared to be a less attractive leader than Mulroney. Polling data in fact shows that having begun the campaign ahead of Mulroney in terms of competence and likeability Turner soon slipped behind his rival.

TABLE 2
Which Leader Would Make the Best PM
(Percentages of Voters)

	Early July	Early August	Late August
Turner	37	26	19
Mulroney	22	29	38

Source: Southam/Carleton Poll

TABLE 3
Which Leader is Liked Best in Personality
(Percentages of Voters)

	Early July	Early August	Late August
Turner	31	23	18
Mulroney	25	32	40

Source: Southam/Carleton Poll (The CBC survey in early August also found Mulroney ahead on competence and personality.)

The question of course is what caused this change of opinion. Jeffrey Simpson in his analysis attaches considerable importance to the leaders' debates on TV on July 23, 24 (in French) and August 15 (on women's issues). Professor Meisel in his analysis of the election has gone further: "If any one factor can be identified as the turning point or causal trigger in the outcome, it was the three debates …More precisely, it was, as we shall see, the aftermath to the debates that was so crucial, even more than the actual exchanges themselves. Together the debates and their shadow epitomized, made concrete and highlighted a wide range of developments and realities and so linked them, in the minds of many, to the voting decision." (3) But polling data suggests that the Liberal decline had begun before the debates, and it may be that among English-speaking Canadians at least, the debates accelerated a trend of opinion already underway. The French debate, however, may well have had an important impact on opinion in Quebec. Most commentators have agreed that Mulroney, in words and style, was better able to identify with Quebec — his home province, after all — than Turner. Southam/Carleton polling data shows that it was in Quebec that the Conservatives made their large gains and the Liberals suffered their sharpest losses among decided voters in the period early-June to early-August.

TABLE 4
Voting Intentions by Region
(Percentages of Decided Voters *)

	Libs.	PC	NDP	Others
ATLANTIC REGION				
Early July before debates	46	45	7	2
Early Aug. after two debates	45	48	7	0
Late Aug. after women's issues debate	32	56	12	0
Election result	34	53	12	1
QUEBEC				
Early July before debates	61	28	4	7
Early Aug. after two debates	37	49	9	5
Late Aug. after women's issues debate	32	56	9	3
Election result	35	50	9	6
ONTARIO				
Early July before debates	45	42	10	3
Early Aug. after two debates	33	49	17	1
Late Aug. after women's issues debate	30	53	16	1
Election result	30	48	21	1
WESTERN REGION				
Early July before debates	32	54	14	0
Early Aug. after two debates	21	56	21	2
Late Aug. after women's issues debate	17	62	20	1
Election result	16	52	28	4

* Percentages may not add to 100 due to rounding.
Source: Southam/Carleton polls taken July 4-12; Aug. 1-7; Aug. 19-2?; and Report of Chief Electoral Officer.

    In the Atlantic region, the first two debates had no immediate effect on voting intentions. The swing to the Conservatives came later, and it cannot convincingly be ascribed to the impact of the third debate, on women's issues, if only because data suggest that the big winner on that occasion was the NDP leader, Broadbent. In Quebec, however, the Liberals were leading in early July — although the Conservatives were running much more strongly than usual. After the first two debates in English and French, many voters who had been intending to vote Liberal moved into the undecided category. The result was that among decided voters the Liberals dropped by an astonishing 24 percentage points; the Conservatives rose by 21 points. The debates were not presumably the only cause, but it is reasonable to assume that the French-language debate was a powerful influence in building on the base of Conservative support previously visible. In Ontario, the Liberals dropped 12 points between July and August, but the Conservatives gained only seven. Given the other factors at work to weaken the Liberals, it cannot be said that the first two debates were decisive. After the debate on women's issues, not a great deal changed in the province. In the West, the Liberals dropped 11 points between July and August, but the Conservatives gained only two. Even making allowance for polling error — the margin is larger when national samples are analysed by region — there appears to have been a swing from Conservatives to NDP in the closing weeks of the campaign. This was perhaps a tribute to the tenacious NDP campaign which has been described by Nick Hills. The West was more anxious than any other region to be rid of the

Liberals, and in the early stages of the campaign even NDP supporters may have planned to vote Conservative to achieve that end. But when it became apparent that the Liberals were indeed going to be heavily defeated, these voters may have felt it no long necessary to support the Conservatives and so returned to the NDP. Somewhat the same thinking could explain the surprising victory of Turner in his own Vancouver riding in the face of earlier polls indicating he would be defeated; with the Liberal party defeated nationally, the voters may have felt free to support Turner personally.

In summary, the TV debates were no doubt important in establishing the images of the leaders, but the evidence does not suggest that they were decisive in forming voting intentions, except perhaps in Quebec. But nor, it appears, was the coverage of the leaders by the news media. The analysis in an earlier chapter shows that at least the leading newspapers were remarkably even-handed in their reporting of , and commentary on, Turner and Mulroney. The story is very different, however, when one examines the coverage of the political parties; the Liberal party had few friends and no admirers in the news media analysed, and it may be that Turner suffered merely by association with that highly unpopular institution.

ISSUES

If there are ever elections in Canada in which policy issues are important in differentiating the parties, this was not one of them. The voters, the news media and the party leaders all agreed that the state of the economy in general and unemployment in particular were the major problems facing the country. But when it came to solutions, there was little to choose between the Liberals and Conservatives. Both Turner and Mulroney promised in vague terms to reduce the budget deficit, improve the efficiency of government, and encourage business enterprise to create growth and jobs. The Liberals tried hard to show that while promising economy, Mulroney was also making lavish spending promises, but that did not impress the voters. There was little to choose also on the so-called national unity issues which in previous elections had worked well for the Liberals; Mulroney was obviously acceptable in Quebec, and in effect he adopted the Liberal position on the status of French in Canada. On the issues of importance to women, Broadbent and the NDP appeared to be the most responsive, but clearly it did not turn into many votes.

Another sort of issue is that which concerns not so much policy as attitude. In this category was the storm about patronage which blew up during the campaign. The events have been described and it is sufficient here to note that while it was cleverly exploited by Mulroney and received great attention in the media, it seems not to have been taken too seriously by the voters: most blamed the former prime minister, Trudeau, rather than Turner for the much-criticized appointments, and in a Southam/Carleton poll, 74 per cent said that all parties would use patronage in much the same way — a judgement vindicated by events when the Conservatives formed the new government. Similarly, there is little evidence that Turner's habit of patting the bottoms of leading Liberal ladies had much effect on the voters despite the attention it received in the media and the suggestion that it showed him to be a man out-of-touch with the new status and sensibilities of women. But if there is not much evidence that these issues worked against Turner, they certainly did not work for him. Mulroney avoided controversy on matters of substance, and Turner was unable to demonstrate that a Conservative government would be less competent or socially progressive than his government. And while issues raised about Turner's style may not individually have been important, as a constellation — patronage, bum-patting, fumbles with facts, an uneasy relationship with the media — they may have formed an unfavorable image in the minds of the voters. In a campaign in which there are no policy issues of substance, image or style become important.

As the analysis of media coverage has shown, more attention was paid to campaign process than to policy. Journalists were keenly interested in the party organizations, and here again the Liberals suffered badly. It was soon apparent that the Liberal campaign organization was far less efficient than that of the Conservatives, and internal dissent became public when Turner fired his campaign manager and recalled the team from the Trudeau era. While this team was highly experienced, it was also seen by many journalists — and indeed by many Liberals — as a symbol of the "bad old days" when the party was run from the Prime Minister's Office which relied on polls and publicity to manipulate public and political opinion. The misadventures of the Liberal party campaign became a major news story in themselves while the Conservative campaign was widely admired, and the NDP campaign escaped any critical reporting, probably because it was not considered to be an important factor in the election.

CONCLUSION

As the review above suggests, no single explanation of the defeat of the Liberals is satisfactory. A number of factors were at work. The Liberals had been in trouble with public opinion for some years before 1984. Their support outside Quebec was eroding, and a desire for a change of government was evident as early as 1979. For a brief period, it appeared as if Turner might be able to supply that change, but soon after he became Prime Minister his connections with the previous Liberal administration and with the ongoing Liberal party undermined his claim to be a man of change. His image as a competent administrator and business leader collapsed, in part because of the inept management of his campaign. The voters quickly returned to their long-held view that the Conservatives offered a better prospect of real change: polling data late in the campaign found that time-for-a-change was the single most important reason for voting decisions. Voters found it easy to switch away from the Liberals because the Conservatives had captured the middle ground. The CBC election poll found that 38 per cent of those surveyed felt that the Conservatives best represented the middle class, as opposed to 25 per cent for the Liberals. On the other hand 49 per cent considered the Liberals the party to be the closest to the rich, as opposed to

25 per cent for the Conservatives. So powerful were the desires for change and a new image of the Conservatives as a party of the centre that they overrode traditional voting patterns, including the loyalty of Quebec to the Liberals.

ENDNOTES

(1) John Meisel, "The Boob-Tube Election", TheWhig-Standard Magazine, Kingston March 2, 1985.
(2) See Table 3, Chapter 4.
(3) Meisel, "The Boob-Tube Election".

TABLE A1
FEDERAL ELECTION RESULTS*
(X = less than 1%)

		1945	1949	1953	1957	1958	1962	1963	1965	1968	1972	1974	1979	1980	1984
LIB	VOTE %	41	49.5	49	41	34	37	41	40	46	39	43	40	44	28
	SEATS	125	193	171	105	49	100	129	131	155	109	141	114	147	40
PC	VOTE %	27	30	31	39	54	37	33	32	31	35	35	36	33	50
	SEATS	67	41	51	112	208	116	95	97	72	107	95	136	103	211
**NDP	VOTE %	16	13	11	11	9.5	13	14	18	17	18	15	18	20	18
	SEATS	28	13	23	25	8	19	17	21	23	31	16	26	32	30
SC	VOTE %	4	4	5	7	3	12	12	8	4	8	5	5	2	1
	SEATS	13	10	15	19	0	30	24	5	14	15	11	6	0	0
OTHER	VOTE %	12	4	3	3	X	1	X	2	2	X	2	1	1	3
	SEATS	12	5	5	4	0	0	0	11	1	2	1	0	0	1
% TURNOUT		75	74	67.5	74	79	79	79	75	76	77	71	76	69	76
CANADA TOTAL NUMBER OF SEATS		245	262	265	265	265	265	265	265	264	264	264	282	282	282

* REPORTS OF THE CHIEF ELECTORAL OFFICER.
** CCF UP TO AND INCLUDING THE 1958 ELECTION.

TABLE A2
ELECTION RESULTS BY PROVINCE 1958 AND 1984*
(X = less than 1%)

		1958				1984			
		LIB	PC	CCF	OTHERS	LIB	PC	NDP	OTHERS
NFLD.	VOTE %	54	45	X	X	36	58	6	X
	SEATS	5	2	0	0	3	4	0	0
P.E.I.	VOTE %	37.5	62	X	X	41	52	6	X
	SEATS	0	4	0	0	1	3	0	0
N.S.	VOTE %	38	57	4.5	X	34	51	15	X
	SEATS	0	12	0	0	2	9	0	0
N.B.	VOTE %	43	54	2	X	32	54	14	X
	SEATS	3	7	0	0	1	9	0	0
QUE.	VOTE %	46	50	2	3	35	50	9	5
	SEATS	25	50	0	0	17	58	0	0
ONT.	VOTE %	33	56	10.5	X	30	48	21	1
	SEATS	15	67	3	0	14	67	13	1
MAN.	VOTE %	22	57	20	2	22	43	27	8
	SEATS	0	14	0	0	1	9	4	0
SASK.	VOTE %	20	51	28	X	18	42	38	2
	SEATS	0	14	1	0	0	9	5	0
ALTA.	VOTE %	14	60	4	22	13	69	14	4
	SEATS	0	17	0	0	0	21	0	0
B.C.	VOTE %	16	49	24.5	10	16	47	35	2
	SEATS	0	18	4	0	1	19	8	0
YUKON/NWT	VOTE %	50	49	X	1	24	47	23	4
	SEATS	1	1	0	0	0	3	0	0
TOTAL	VOTE %	34	54	9.5	3	28	50	19	3
	SEATS	49	208	8	0	40	211	30	1

* REPORTS OF THE CHIEF ELECTORAL OFFICER

TABLE A3
ELECTION RESULTS BY REGION 1945-1984 (SEATS)*

	1945	1949	1953	1957	1958	1962	1963	1965	1968	1972	1974	1979	1980	1984
ATLANTIC														
LIB	19	25	27	12	8	14	20	15	7	10	13	12	19	7
PC	6	7	5	21	25	18	13	18	25	22	17	18	13	25
CCF/NDP	1	1	1	—	—	1	—	—	—	—	1	2	0	—
SC	—	—	—	—	—	—	—	—	—	—	—	—	—	—
OTHER	1	1	—	—	—	—	—	—	—	—	1	—	—	—
TOTAL	27	34	33	33	33	33	33	33	32	32	32	32	32	32
QUEBEC														
LIB	53	66	66	63	25	35	47	56	56	56	60	67	74	17
PC	2	2	4	9	50	14	8	8	4	2	3	2	1	58
CCF/NDP	—	—	—	—	—	—	—	—	—	—	—	—	—	—
SC	—	—	—	—	—	26	20	9	14	15	11	6	—	—
OTHER	10	5	5	3	—	—	—	2	—	1	—	—	—	—
TOTAL	65	73	75	75	75	75	75	75	74	74	74	75	75	75
ONTARIO														
LIB	34	56	50	20	14	43	52	51	64	36	55	32	52	14
PC	48	25	33	61	67	35	27	25	17	40	25	57	38	67
CCF/NDP	—	1	1	3	3	6	6	9	6	11	8	6	5	13
SC	—	—	—	—	—	—	—	—	—	—	—	—	—	—
OTHER	—	—	—	—	—	—	—	—	1	1	—	—	—	1
TOTAL	82	83	85	85	85	85	85	85	88	88	88	95	95	95
WEST														
LIB	19	43	27	10	1	7	10	9	29	7	13	3	2	2
PC	11	7	9	21	66	49	47	46	25	43	50	57	49	58
CCF/NDP	27	10	21	22	5	12	11	12	16	20	7	17	26	17
SC	13	10	15	19	—	4	4	5	—	—	—	—	—	—
OTHER	1	1	—	—	—	—	—	—	—	—	—	—	—	—
TOTAL	71	71	72	72	72	72	72	72	70	70	70	77	77	77

* REPORTS OF THE CHIEF ELECTORAL OFFICER

TABLE A4
ELECTION RESULTS BY PROVINCE 1974-1984*
(X = less than 1%)

	LIBERAL				PC				NDP				ALL OTHERS			
	1984	1980	1979	1974	1984	1980	1979	1974	1984	1980	1979	1974	1984	1980	1979	1974
NFLD.																
VOTE %	36	47	38	47	58	36	31	44	6	17	31	9	X	X	X	X
SEATS	3	5	4	4	4	2	2	3	0	0	1	0	0	0	0	0
P.E.I.																
VOTE %	41	47	40	46	52	46	53	49	6	7	7	5	X	X	X	X
SEATS	1	2	0	1	3	2	4	3	0	0	0	0	0	0	0	0
N.S.																
VOTE %	34	40	36	41	51	39	45	47	15	21	19	11	X	X	X	X
SEATS	2	5	2	2	9	6	8	8	0	0	1	1	0	0	0	0
N.B.																
VOTE %	32	50	45	47	54	33	40	33	14	16	15	9	X	X	X	11
SEATS	1	7	6	6	9	3	4	3	0	0	0	0	0	0	0	1
QUEBEC																
VOTE %	35	68	62	54	50	13	13	21	9	9	5	7	5	10	20	18
SEATS	17	74	67	60	58	1	2	3	0	0	0	0	0	0	6	11
ONTARIO																
VOTE %	30	42	37	45	48	36	42	35	21	22	21	19	1	X	1	1
SEATS	14	52	32	55	67	38	57	25	13	5	6	8	1	0	0	0
MAN.																
VOTE %	22	28	24	27	43	38	44	48	27	34	33	24	8	X	X	1
SEATS	1	2	2	2	9	5	7	9	4	7	5	2	0	0	0	0
SASK.																
VOTE %	18	24	20	31	42	39	42	36	38	36	37	32	2	1	1	1
SEATS	0	0	0	3	9	7	10	8	5	0	4	2	0	0	0	0
ALTA.																
VOTE %	13	21	21	25	69	66	67	61	14	10	10	9	4	3	3	5
SEATS	0	0	0	0	21	21	21	19	0	0	0	0	0	0	0	0

Table A4 (continued)

ELECTION RESULTS BY PROVINCE 1974-1984*

(X = less than 1%)

	LIBERAL				PC				NDP				ALL OTHERS			
	1984	1980	1979	1974	1984	1980	1979	1974	1984	1980	1979	1974	1984	1980	1979	1974
B.C.																
VOTE %	16	22	23	33	47	41	45	42	35	35	32	23	2	2	1	2
SEATS	1	0	1	8	19	16	20	12	8	12	8	2	0	0	0	0
YUKON/NWT																
VOTE %	24	37	33	28	47	32	37	39	23	31	29	33	4	X	1	X
SEATS	0	0	0	0	3	2	2	1	0	1	1	1	0	0	0	0
CANADA TOTAL																
VOTE %	28	44	40	43	50	33	36	35	19	20	18	15	3	3	6	6
SEATS	40	147	114	141	211	103	136	95	30	32	26	16	1	0	6	12

* REPORTS OF THE CHIEF ELECTORAL OFFICER

CONSTITUENCY* RESULTS	1984	1980
KEY		
PC	PROGRESSIVE CONSERVATIVES	
LIB	LIBERALS	
NDP	NEW DEMOCRATIC PARTY	
RHINO	RHINOCEROS PARTY	
LIBERT	LIBERTARIAN	
COMM	COMMUNIST PARTY OF CANADA	
M-L	MARXIST-LENINIST	
SC	SOCIAL CREDIT	
GREEN	GREEN PARTY/LE PARTI VERT	
COMMONWEALTH	PARTY FOR COMMON-WEALTH/ PARTI POUR REPUBLIQUE	
CONFED RWP	CONFEDERATION OF REGIONS WESTERN PARTY	
PN	PARTI NATIONALISTE DE QUEBEC	
UP	UNION POPULAIRE	
IND	INDEPENDENT	

ONTARIO ALGOMA	1984	1980
PC	34.7%	16.3%
LIB	38.3%	50.5%
NDP	25.8%	32.7%
NO AFFILIATION	1.3%	—
LIBERT	—	.3%
M-L	—	.1%
TOTAL	36,885	34,489

BRAMPTON-GEORGETOWN	1984	1980
PC	56.2%	40.5%
LIB	27.4%	39.9%
NDP	15.7%	19.2%
GREEN	.5%	—
LIBERT	—	.3%
COMM	.2%	.1%
M-L	—	.1%
TOTAL	85,035	62,402

BRANT	1984	1980
PC	41.5%	31.3%
LIB	13.9%	27.3%
NDP	44.2%	41.1%

CONSTITUENCY RESULTS	1984	1980
SC	.4%	.2%
M-L	—	.1%
TOTAL	52,275	46,680

BRUCE-GREY	1984	1980
PC	64.7%	47.3%
LIB	23.3%	40.6%
NDP	12.0%	11.3%
LIBERT	—	.8%
TOTAL	42,654	38,751

BURLINGTON	1984	1980
PC	61.9%	50.8%
LIB	18.8%	32.8%
NDP	19.3%	15.7%
LIBERT	—	.6%
M-L	—	.1%
TOTAL	60,670	53,611

CAMBRIDGE	1984	1980
PC	60.2%	39.4%
LIB	14.5%	29.0%
NDP	24.1%	31.2%
RHINO	.9%	—
COMMONWEALTH	.3%	—
SC	—	.3%
M-L	—	.2%
TOTAL	38,134	36,376

COCHRANE-SUPERIOR	1984	1980
PC	32.4%	9.8%
LIB	41.7%	52.6%
NDP	25.9%	37.2%
M-L	—	.4%
TOTAL	29,621	29,062

DURHAM-NORTHUMBERLAND	1984	1980
PC	59.3%	45.1%
LIB	20.8%	29.7%
NDP	18.6%	24.2%
LIBERT	.5%	1.0%
RHINO	.8%	—
M-L	—	0.0%
TOTAL	42,077	39,017

ELGIN	1984	1980
PC	67.1%	49.8%
LIB	19.6%	36.7%
NDP	13.4%	13.3%
M-L	—	.2%
TOTAL	34,745	33,820

ERIE	1984	1980
PC	55.8%	40.0%
LIB	27.1%	38.4%

CONSTITUENCY RESULTS	1984	1980
NDP	17.1%	21.3%
M-L	—	.3%
TOTAL	34,381	32,148
ESSEX-KENT	1984	1980
PC	58.0%	31.1%
LIB	28.8%	53.0%
NDP	13.2%	16.0%
TOTAL	32,163	31,911
ESSEX-WINDSOR	1984	1980
PC	31.6%	8.7%
LIB	29.1%	51.3%
NDP	39.3%	39.8%
M-L	—	.2%
TOTAL	47,685	48,061
GLENGARRY-PRESCOTT-RUSSELL	1984	1980
PC	33.0%	19.7%
LIB	53.1%	68.5%
NDP	13.9%	11.6%
M-L	—	.2%
TOTAL	49,065	41,173
GREY-SIMCOE	1984	1980
PC	59.8%	46.1%
LIB	24.0%	35.1%
NDP	15.4%	17.4%
LIBERT	.9%	1.1%
SC	—	.3%
TOTAL	39,049	35,774
GUELPH	1984	1980
PC	49.9%	37.6%
LIB	29.2%	39.2%
NDP	19.5%	22.2%
RHINO	.7%	.6%
LIBERT	.7%	.2%
M-L	—	.1%
COMM	—	.1%
TOTAL	47,051	44,045
HALDIMAND-NORFOLK	1984	1980
PC	59.0%	42.0%
LIB	26.3%	41.7%
NDP	13.3%	15.7%
IND	1.4%	—
SC	—	.6%
TOTAL	46,251	44,282
HALTON	1984	1980
PC	60.6%	46.8%
LIB	22.5%	36.6%
NDP	14.6%	16.0%
LIBERT	—	.3%
IND	—	.3%
GREEN	2.4%	—

CONSTITUENCY RESULTS	1984	1980
M-L	—	0.0%
TOTAL	62,859	52,917
HAMILTON EAST	1984	1980
PC	30.5%	23.3%
LIB	37.9%	41.8%
NDP	31.0%	34.2%
COMM	.2%	.4%
SC	.3%	—
COMMONWEALTH	.2%	—
No Affiliation	—	.2%
M-L	—	.1%
TOTAL	38,364	36,908
HAMILTON MOUNTAIN	1984	1980
PC	32.4%	32.5%
LIB	18.2%	31.8%
NDP	49.2%	35.5%
COMMONWEALTH	.2%	—
COMM	—	.1%
M-L	—	.1%
TOTAL	52,420	49,903
HAMILTON-WENTWORTH	1984	1980
PC	52.0%	45.0%
LIB	28.8%	32.6%
NDP	18.0%	22.3%
GREEN	.7%	—
LIBERT	.4%	—
COMMONWEALTH	.2%	—
M-L	—	.1%
TOTAL	49,217	42,060
HAMILTON WEST	1984	1980
PC	40.4%	38.6%
LIB	30.2%	37.1%
NDP	28.0%	23.2%
RHINO	—	.8%
LIBERT	.7%	—
COMM	.4%	—
COMMONWEALTH	.3%	—
M-L	—	.4%
TOTAL	41,052	40,202
HASTINGS-FRONTENAC-LENNOX AND ADDINGTON	1984	1980
PC	56.3%	42.3%
LIB	27.5%	39.1%
NDP	15.1%	17.6%
IND	1.2%	—
NO AFFILIATION	—	1.0%
TOTAL	35,543	33,580
HURON-BRUCE	1984	1980
PC	64.8%	47.5%
LIB	23.8%	41.3%

CONSTITUENCY RESULTS	1984	1980
NDP	11.0%	11.1%
LIBERT	.4%	—
TOTAL	37,004	34,748

KENORA-RAINY RIVER	1984	1980
PC	35.3%	16.1%
LIB	27.6%	42.3%
NDP	37.1%	41.3%
M-L	—	.4%
TOTAL	35,946	34,701

KENT	1984	1980
PC	48.8%	40.6%
LIB	34.8%	43.0%
NDP	16.4%	16.4%
TOTAL	37,444	35,191

KINGSTON AND THE ISLANDS	1984	1980
PC	55.1%	41.8%
LIB	27.7%	39.3%
NDP	12.6%	18.1%
NO AFFILIATION	3.0%	—
GREEN	1.0%	—
RHINO	—	.9%
LIBERT	.6%	—
TOTAL	47,180	43,388

KITCHENER	1984	1980
PC	46.8%	36.2%
LIB	28.3%	39.3%
NDP	24.3%	23.2%
LIBERT	.5%	.6%
RHINO	—	.6%
M-L	—	.1%
TOTAL	57,019	49,646

LAMBTON-MIDDLESEX	1984	1980
PC	54.6%	42.9%
LIB	33.7%	45.0%
NDP	11.7%	12.2%
TOTAL	41,215	37,972

LANARK-RENFREW-CARLETON	1984	1980
PC	53.8%	54.6%
LIB	34.2%	31.5%
NDP	11.7%	13.2%
NO AFFILIATION	—	.7%
COMMONWEALTH	.3%	—
TOTAL	45,372	37,499

LEEDS-GRENVILLE	1984	1980
PC	61.5%	51.2%
LIB	23.3%	31.7%
NDP	14.0%	17.1%

CONSTITUENCY RESULTS	1984	1980
GREEN	.8%	—
LIBERT	.4%	—
TOTAL	43,842	38,660

LINCOLN	1984	1980
PC	49.1%	35.0%
LIB	27.3%	36.5%
NDP	22.2%	28.2%
GREEN	.6%	—
SC	.2%	—
IND	.2%	—
NO AFFILIATION	.3%	—
M-L	—	.3%
TOTAL	53,609	47,823

LONDON EAST	1984	1980
PC	47.2%	29.7%
LIB	25.9%	48.1%
NDP	26.9%	21.7%
LIBERT	—	.5%
M-L	—	.1%
TOTAL	38,426	37,175

LONDON-MIDDLESEX	1984	1980
PC	47.0%	32.6%
LIB	28.3%	43.0%
NDP	24.7%	23.8%
LIBERT	—	.4%
M-L	—	.1%
TOTAL	39,541	36,454

LONDON WEST	1984	1980
PC	51.4%	40.8%
LIB	32.3%	44.2%
NDP	16.3%	14.4%
RHINO	—	.4%
LIBERT	—	.3%
M-L	—	.1%
TOTAL	67,129	61,384

MISSISSAUGA NORTH	1984	1980
PC	49.5%	37.9%
LIB	34.9%	44.2%
NDP	14.5%	17.3%
GREEN	.6%	—
LIBERT	.5%	.5%
M-L	—	.1%
TOTAL	95,194	67,848

MISSISSAUGA SOUTH	1984	1980
PC	56.4%	41.4%
LIB	28.9%	40.6%
NDP	14.7%	16.8%
LIBERT	—	.8%
IND	—	.2%
NO AFFILIATION	—	.2%
M-L	—	.1%
TOTAL	58,404	51,892

CONSTITUENCY RESULTS	1984	1980
NEPEAN-CARLETON	1984	1980
PC	55.9%	53.6%
LIB	28.0%	33.1%
NDP	14.8%	12.2%
RHINO	—	1.1%
GREEN	1.0%	—
IND	.3%	—
TOTAL	74,491	58,825
NIAGARA FALLS	1984	1980
PC	55.1%	37.0%
LIB	19.8%	41.2%
NDP	23.8%	21.2%
GREEN	.9%	—
SC	.4%	.6%
M-L	—	.2%
TOTAL	41,463	38,571
NICKEL BELT	1984	1980
PC	31.2%	10.2%
LIB	29.6%	47.5%
NDP	38.6%	42.1%
RHINO	.7%	—
M-L	—	.2%
TOTAL	44,410	41,673
NIPISSING	1984	1980
PC	47.2%	35.8%
LIB	39.8%	50.3%
NDP	13.0%	13.9%
TOTAL	36,540	32,570
NORTHUMBERLAND	1984	1980
PC	62.3%	48.4%
LIB	24.7%	37.7%
NDP	12.0%	13.9%
LIBERT	.4%	—
GREEN	.7%	—
TOTAL	38,627	36,893
ONTARIO	1984	1980
PC	56.1%	40.9%
LIB	23.2%	31.7%
NDP	20.7%	26.2%
RHINO	—	.6%
LIBERT	—	.4%
M-L	—	.1%
TOTAL	62,677	48,835
OSHAWA	1984	1980
PC	38.8%	28.3%
LIB	18.1%	19.6%
NDP	42.3%	51.6%
LIBERT	.6%	.3%
COMMONWEALTH	.1%	—
COMM	.1%	.2%
M-L	—	.1%
TOTAL	59,320	51,823

CONSTITUENCY RESULTS	1984	1980
OTTAWA-CARLETON	1984	1984
PC	44.7%	34.2%
LIB	39.7%	53.5%
NDP	13.9%	11.9%
RHINO	.8%	—
IND	.4%	—
GREEN	.4%	—
NO AFFILIATION	—	.4%
COMMONWEALTH	.1%	—
TOTAL	77,539	65,367
OTTAWA CENTRE	1984	1980
PC	34.3%	36.4%
LIB	29.6%	45.9%
NDP	34.4%	16.0%
RHINO	.7%	.8%
GREEN	.6%	—
NO AFFILIATION	—	.4%
NO AFFILIATION	—	.1%
COMM	.2%	.3%
IND	.1%	.1%
IND	.1%	.1%
IND	.1%	—
M-L	—	.1%
TOTAL	51,919	47,187
OTTAWA-VANIER	1984	1980
PC	28.8%	17.8%
LIB	49.1%	66.5%
NDP	21.5%	13.8%
RHINO	—	1.3%
IND	.6%	—
NO AFFILIATION	—	.4%
M-L	—	.2%
TOTAL	43,601	41,449
OTTAWA WEST	1984	1980
PC	48.8%	43.2%
LIB	35.4%	44.3%
NDP	15.2%	11.7%
IND	.5%	.8%
TOTAL	54,494	50,753
OXFORD	1984	1980
PC	57.1%	45.9%
LIB	28.7%	36.8%
NDP	13.5%	16.3%
LIBERT	.7%	.7%
M-L	—	.2%
TOTAL	44,925	42,224
PARRY SOUND-MUSKOKA	1984	1980
PC	57.2%	42.1%
LIB	24.1%	35.6%
NDP	17.9%	22.3%
IND	.8%	—
TOTAL	39,723	34,085

CONSTITUENCY RESULTS	1984	1980
PERTH	1984	1980
PC	54.9%	47.5%
LIB	29.1%	37.8%
NDP	16.0%	14.5%
M-L	—	.2%
TOTAL	34,940	31,940
PETERBOROUGH	1984	1980
PC	52.7%	40.3%
LIB	22.8%	35.7%
NDP	20.7%	22.3%
LIBERT	2.9%	1.0%
RHINO	.6%	.5%
IND	.3%	—
IND	—	.1%
M-L	—	.1%
TOTAL	51,469	48,243
PRINCE EDWARD-HASTINGS	1984	1980
PC	54.3%	45.9%
LIB	26.7%	34.8%
NDP	18.5%	18.7%
IND	.5%	.6%
TOTAL	38,714	36,814
RENFREW-NIPISSING-PEMBROKE	1984	1980
PC	45.0%	32.7%
LIB	45.1%	51.7%
NDP	9.8%	15.6%
TOTAL	43,219	39,695
ST. CATHARINES	1984	1980
PC	49.7%	37.9%
LIB	18.5%	35.0%
NDP	30.6%	26.5%
GREEN	.7%	—
RHINO	—	.5%
COMM	.2%	.2%
SC	.2%	—
COMMONWEALTH	.1%	—
M-L	—	.1%
TOTAL	53,530	49,142
SARNIA-LAMBTON	1984	1980
PC	54.6%	34.9%
LIB	25.7%	40.6%
NDP	19.4%	24.5%
IND	.2%	—
IND	.1%	—
M-L	—	.1%
TOTAL	44,058	40,122
SAULT STE. MARIE	1984	1980
PC	38.6%	12.9%
LIB	29.3%	48.0%
NDP	31.5%	38.9%
COMMONWEALTH	.6%	—

CONSTITUENCY RESULTS	1984	1980
M-L	—	.2%
TOTAL	34,031	32,211
SIMCOE NORTH	1984	1980
PC	55.0%	36.4%
LIB	26.6%	36.3%
NDP	17.1%	27.3%
GREEN	.8%	—
LIBERT	.5%	—
TOTAL	45,282	40,821
SIMCOE SOUTH	1984	1980
PC	58.1%	43.5%
LIB	26.3%	35.6%
NDP	15.7%	20.9%
TOTAL	52,891	45,416
STORMONT-DUNDAS	1984	1980
PC	46.0%	36.0%
LIB	41.2%	53.0%
NDP	12.8%	11.0%
TOTAL	45,733	41,969
SUDBURY	1984	1980
PC	32.3%	11.8%
LIB	41.3%	55.7%
NDP	25.7%	31.2%
RHINO	.6%	.7%
COMM	.2%	.2%
M-L	—	.2%
NO AFFILIATION	—	.2%
TOTAL	43,613	39,417
THUNDER BAY-ATIKOKAN	1984	1980
PC	34.0%	21.4%
LIB	24.6%	39.2%
NDP	41.5%	39.0%
LIBERT	—	.3%
M-L	—	.1%
TOTAL	35,459	33,731
THUNDER BAY-NIPIGON	1984	1980
PC	28.3%	16.5%
LIB	34.0%	46.6%
NDP	37.2%	36.4%
LIBERT	.5%	—
COMM	—	.3%
M-L	—	.2%
TOTAL	37,418	35,584
TIMISKAMING	1984	1980
PC	53.9%	18.3%
LIB	22.1%	41.6%
NDP	23.5%	39.8%
SC	.5%	—
M-L	—	.4%
TOTAL	28,503	26,790

CONSTITUENCY RESULTS	1984	1980
TIMMINS-CHAPLEAU	1984	1980
PC	37.5%	12.2%
LIB	32.2%	51.9%
NDP	29.9%	35.7%
NO AFFILIATION	.4%	—
M-L	—	.2%
TOTAL	31,887	30,093
VICTORIA-HALIBURTON	1984	1980
PC	60.9%	48.4%
LIB	20.2%	29.5%
NDP	17.5%	21.2%
LIBERT	.7%	.9%
GREEN	.7%	—
TOTAL	49,606	41,947
WATERLOO	1984	1980
PC	56.4%	40.0%
LIB	24.6%	39.7%
NDP	18.2%	19.1%
LIBERT	.9%	.4%
RHINO	—	.6%
M-L	—	.2%
TOTAL	56,608	51,529
WELLAND	1984	1980
PC	42.0%	27.3%
LIB	33.0%	43.9%
NDP	24.0%	28.4%
GREEN	.7%	—
COMM	.3%	.2%
M-L	—	.2%
TOTAL	43,836	41,306
WELLINGTON-DUFFERIN-SIMCOE	1984	1980
PC	68.5%	53.8%
LIB	16.7%	30.7%
NDP	14.8%	15.1%
LIBERT	—	.4%
TOTAL	43,754	39,437
WINDSOR-WALKERVILLE	1984	1980
PC	34.1%	11.4%
LIB	29.1%	52.0%
NDP	36.8%	36.0%
COMM	—	.4%
M-L	—	.2%
TOTAL	39,724	40,119
WINDSOR WEST	1984	1980
PC	24.3%	12.2%
LIB	40.6%	58.5%
NDP	34.2%	29.0%
COMM	—	.2%
RHINO	.7%	—

CONSTITUENCY RESULTS	1984	1980
COMM	.3%	—
M-L	—	.2%
TOTAL	33,601	33,768
YORK NORTH	1984	1980
PC	31.7%	43.5%
LIB	20.4%	40.6%
NDP	11.4%	14.9%
NO AFFILIATION	36.5%	—
LIBERT	—	.9%
M-L	—	.1%
TOTAL	88,266	59,846
YORK-PEEL	1984	1980
PC	62.2%	47.1%
LIB	20.8%	34.0%
NDP	15.5%	17.1%
RHINO	—	1.2%
IND	.8%	—
LIBERT	.7%	.6%
TOTAL	60,301	50,872
METROPOLITAN TORONTO BEACHES	1984	1980
PC	33.9%	31.4%
LIB	22.2%	31.3%
NDP	40.6%	35.6%
GREEN	1.6%	—
LIBERT	1.0%	.8%
RHINO	—	.6%
IND	.4%	.1%
NO AFFILIATION	.3%	—
COMMONWEALTH	.1%	—
M-L	—	.2%
TOTAL	36,717	35,564
BROADVIEW-GREENWOOD	1984	1980
PC	34.7%	23.9%
LIB	18.3%	33.0%
NDP	45.6%	40.4%
LIBERT	—	1.1%
RHINO	.7%	.6%
GREEN	.7%	—
COMM	—	.5%
NO AFFILIATION	—	.2%
M-L	—	.2%
IND	—	.1%
TOTAL	33,044	32,089
DAVENPORT	1984	1980
PC	21.1%	13.6%
LIB	53.7%	62.4%
NDP	22.5%	22.2%
LIBERT	1.0%	1.0%
GREEN	1.0%	—
COMM	.7%	.5%
M-L	—	.3%
TOTAL	24,686	23,301

CONSTITUENCY RESULTS	1984	1980
DON VALLEY EAST	1984	1980
PC	54.4%	42.9%
LIB	34.0%	44.6%
NDP	10.7%	11.6%
LIBERT	.7%	.6%
IND	.3%	.2%
M-L	—	.1%
TOTAL	54,644	49,200
DON VALLEY WEST	1984	1980
PC	59.9%	51.8%
LIB	25.8%	37.8%
NDP	13.2%	9.6%
LIBERT	1.2%	.8%
M-L	—	.1%
TOTAL	49,907	48,799
EGLINTON-LAWRENCE	1984	1980
PC	40.3%	33.8%
LIB	43.0%	50.5%
NDP	14.9%	14.7%
LIBERT	.8%	.8%
IND	.5%	—
COMM	.5%	—
M-L	—	.2%
TOTAL	43,379	41,337
ETOBICOKE CENTRE	1984	1980
PC	56.8%	47.1%
LIB	29.8%	41.4%
NDP	12.8%	10.8%
LIBERT	.6%	.5%
M-L	—	.2%
TOTAL	59,875	57,261
ETOBICOKE-LAKESHORE	1984	1980
PC	44.8%	30.1%
LIB	30.3%	40.8%
NDP	23.7%	28.3%
LIBERT	.7%	.6%
COMM	.5%	—
M-L	—	.2%
TOTAL	44,439	43,852
ETOBICOKE NORTH	1984	1980
PC	40.5%	31.9%
LIB	38.9%	46.4%
NDP	19.9%	20.4%
LIBERT	.7%	1.1%
NO AFFILIATION	—	.1%
M-L	—	.2%
TOTAL	56,106	50,082
PARKDALE-HIGH PARK	1984	1980
PC	40.2%	32.1%
LIB	36.5%	45.6%

CONSTITUENCY RESULTS	1984	1980
NDP	20.9%	21.4%
GREEN	1.5%	—
LIBERT	.6%	.4%
COMM	.3%	.4%
M-L	—	.2%
TOTAL	39,475	37,784
ROSEDALE	1984	1980
PC	52.8%	44.0%
LIB	26.1%	39.1%
NDP	17.8%	14.9%
GREEN	1.9%	—
RHINO	—	.8%
LIBERT	.7%	.4%
COMM	.4%	.2%
COMMONWEALTH	.3%	—
IND	—	.3%
NO AFFILIATION	—	.3%
M-L	—	.1%
TOTAL	43,963	38,360
ST. PAUL'S	1984	1980
PC	47.6%	39.5%
LIB	37.9%	45.3%
NDP	12.6%	13.4%
GREEN	1.2%	—
RHINO	—	.8%
LIBERT	.5%	.4%
NO AFFILIATION	—	.3%
COMM	.2%	.2%
COMMONWEALTH	.1%	—
IND	—	.1%
M-L	—	.1%
TOTAL	43,977	39,565
SCARBOROUGH CENTRE	1984	1980
PC	46.7%	36.4%
LIB	33.3%	40.3%
NDP	19.3%	22.4%
LIBERT	.8%	.6%
M-L	—	.2%
TOTAL	42,782	41,162
SCARBOROUGH EAST	1984	1980
PC	55.6%	40.5%
LIB	28.1%	39.4%
NDP	13.6%	19.6%
GREEN	1.2%	—
LIBERT	1.1%	.4%
COMM	.3%	—
COMMONWEALTH	.2%	—
M-L	—	.1%
TOTAL	47,390	43,579
SCARBOROUGH WEST	1984	1980
PC	40.9%	31.3%
LIB	29.4%	35.1%

CONSTITUENCY RESULTS	1984	1980
NDP	27.5%	32.3%
LIBERT	.8%	1.0%
GREEN	.9%	—
COMMONWEALTH	.3%	—
COMM	.2%	.2%
M-L	—	.2%
TOTAL	41,616	40,765
SPADINA	1984	1980
PC	23.8%	20.9%
LIB	35.0%	46.8%
NDP	39.0%	29.0%
LIBERT	1.1%	.8%
RHINO	.9%	.9%
RHINO	—	.5%
COMM	—	.3%
IND	.3%	.1%
NO AFFILIATION	—	.2%
NO AFFILIATION	—	.3%
M-L	—	.2%
TOTAL	33,927	28,385
TRINITY	1984	1980
PC	22.8%	16.8%
LIB	43.6%	57.5%
NDP	29.8%	22.8%
LIBERT	1.1%	1.9%
GREEN	1.5%	—
COMM	.9%	.7%
COMMONWEALTH	.3%	—
M-L	—	.3%
TOTAL	22,507	21,956
WILLOWDALE	1984	1980
PC	43.5%	37.4%
LIB	42.8%	47.4%
NDP	13.0%	14.7%
LIBERT	.6%	.4%
M-L	—	.1%
TOTAL	51,528	46,867
YORK CENTRE	1984	1980
PC	27.4%	17.8%
LIB	51.2%	61.0%
NDP	19.8%	20.3%
LIBERT	.6%	.8%
NO AFFILIATION	.6%	—
NO AFFILIATION	.5%	—
M-L	—	.2%
TOTAL	40,658	37,918
YORK EAST	1984	1980
PC	47.3%	36.3%
LIB	35.5%	44.9%
NDP	16.3%	17.4%
LIBERT	.5%	.8%
RHINO	—	.5%
COMM	.4%	—
M-L	—	.1%
TOTAL	46,492	45,887

CONSTITUENCY RESULTS	1984	1980
YORK-SCARBOROUGH	1984	1980
PC	48.6%	37.8%
LIB	35.7%	47.9%
NDP	13.2%	13.4%
LIBERT	1.1%	.4%
IND	.7%	.5%
IND	.7%	—
M-L	—	.1%
TOTAL	100,375	81,839
YORK SOUTH-WESTON	1984	1980
PC	28.6%	24.9%
LIB	37.7%	47.2%
NDP	31.0%	26.5%
NO AFFILIATION	1.4%	—
LIBERT	.8%	.9%
COMM	.5%	.3%
M-L	—	.2%
TOTAL	37,666	34,991
YORK WEST	1984	1980
PC	30.9%	18.9%
LIB	44.6%	56.8%
NDP	22.0%	23.6%
LIBERT	.9%	.5%
IND	.7%	—
GREEN	.6%	—
COMM	.4%	.2%
M-L	—	.1%
TOTAL	39,564	37,678
QUEBEC		
ABITIBI	1984	1980
PC	52.0%	4.6%
LIB	28.0%	51.1%
NDP	8.0%	5.9%
SC	2.6%	34.5%
RHINO	5.1%	—
PN	4.3%	—
IND	—	2.3%
UP	—	1.0%
M-L	—	.7%
TOTAL	44,706	43,190
ARGENTEUIL-PAPINEAU	1984	1980
PC	55.9%	16.0%
LIB	32.1%	68.6%
NDP	7.1%	7.6%
RHINO	2.5%	4.1%
SC	—	3.4%
PN	1.5%	—
IND	.9%	—
M-L	—	.4%
TOTAL	37,734	32,033
BEAUCE	1984	1980
PC	53.1%	1.9%

CONSTITUENCY RESULTS	1984	1980
LIB	43.1%	50.9%
NDP	2.6%	1.0%
SC	—	44.0%
RHINO	—	1.5%
PN	1.2%	—
IND	—	.7%
M-L	—	.1%
TOTAL	47,137	42,542

BEAUHARNOIS-SALABERRY	1984	1980
PC	63.1%	15.0%
LIB	26.1%	73.1%
NDP	6.2%	7.3%
RHINO	2.8%	—
SC	—	2.7%
PN	1.8%	—
NO AFFILIATION	—	1.1%
UP	—	.6%
M-L	—	.2%
TOTAL	43,743	37,564

BELLECHASSE	1984	1980
PC	57.8%	7.2%
LIB	34.4%	51.1%
NDP	4.0%	1.8%
SC	—	37.5%
RHINO	2.5%	2.0%
PN	1.2%	—
UP	—	.4%
TOTAL	42,111	40,358

BERTHIER-MASKINONGE-LANAUDIERE	1984	1980
PC	69.6%	43.4%
LIB	26.2%	52.7%
NDP	2.7%	—
RHINO	—	1.8%
PN	1.4%	—
SC	—	1.4%
UP	—	.3%
M-L	—	.4%
COMMONWEALTH	.2%	—
TOTAL	44,801	40,267

BLAINVILLE-DEUX-MONTAGNES	1984	1980
PC	47.1%	7.1%
LIB	38.8%	74.0%
NDP	9.2%	11.2%
RHINO	2.5%	3.5%
SC	0.4%	3.5%
PN	1.7%	—
M-L	—	.1%
UP	—	.4%
LIBERT	—	.2%
NO AFFILIATION	.2%	-
COMMONWEALTH	.1%	-
IND	0.0%	-
TOTAL	61,246	48,615

CONSTITUENCY RESULTS	1984	1980
BONAVENTURE-ILES-DE-LA-MADELEINE	**1984**	**1980**
PC	50.1%	18.3%
LIB	44.2%	69.4%
NDP	3.4%	5.7%
PRNHINO	—	1.4%
PN	1.4%	—
SC	—	1.9%
RHINO	—	3.3%
COMMONWEALTH	.9%	—
TOTAL	30,951	27,660

BROME-MISSISQUOI	1984	1980
PC	53.1%	40.9%
LIB	38.4%	53.1%
NDP	5.6%	4..0%
RHINO	—	1.8%
LIBERT	.3%	—
PN	2.4%	—
COMMONWEALTH	.2%	—
M-L	—	.2%
TOTAL	40,851	37,719

CHAMBLY	1984	1980
PC	51.8%	9.9%
LIB	29.7%	69.9%
NDP	11.2%	12.5%
RHINO	3.8%	3.7%
SC	—	3.4%
PN	3.2%	—
COMMONWEALTH	.3%	—
UP	—	.5%
M-L	—	.3%
TOTAL	60,855	47,021

CHAMPLAIN	1984	1980
PC	60.0%	11.0%
LIB	31.6%	64.9%
NDP	6.8%	23.1%
PN	1.6%	—
UP	—	.6%
M-L	—	.5%
TOTAL	45,773	39,697

CHARLESBOURG	1984	1980
PC	52.4%	6.9%
LIB	31.6%	71.1%
NDP	10.2%	12.3%
RHINO	3.6%	5.1%
SC	.7%	3.8%
PN	1.5%	—
COMMONWEALTH	.1%	—
UP	—	.8%
TOTAL	71,728	59,906

CHARLEVOIX	1984	1980
PC	63.6%	18.2%
LIB	32.0%	70.8%
NDP	2.8%	4.1%

CONSTITUENCY RESULTS	1984	1980
PN	1.6%	—
RHINO	—	3.0%
SC	—	3.3%
UP	—	.7%
TOTAL	37,199	31,280
CHATEAUGUAY	1984	1980
PC	46.6%	9.0%
LIB	37.8%	74.2%
NDP	11.1%	11.5%
PN	3.6%	—
COMMONWEALTH	.3%	—
LIBERT	.6%	—
SC	—	3.2%
UP	—	1.6%
M-L	—	.5%
TOTAL	45,752	36,617
CHICOUTIMI	1984	1980
PC	60.8%	18.2%
LIB	29.3%	67.5%
NDP	6.0%	9.5%
SC	—	3.6%
RHINO	2.2%	—
PN	1.7%	—
UP	—	1.2%
TOTA	36,678	30,839
DRUMMOND	1984	1980
PC	56.2%	14.7%
LIB	33.6%	72.8%
NDP	6.2%	6.4%
SC	.7%	5.4%
PN	2.5%	—
NO AFFILIATION	.8%	—
UP	—	.5%
M-L	—	.3%
TOTAL	42,136	35,845
FRONTENAC	1984	1980
PC	71.2%	15.3%
LIB	23.1%	45.9%
NDP	2.7%	5.3%
SC	—	32.2%
RHINO	2.1%	—
PN	1.0%	—
NO AFFILIATION	—	.6%
IND	—	.3%
IND	—	.3%
M-L	—	.1%
TOTAL	39,690	32,129
GASPE	1984	1980
PC	60.9%	32.6%
LIB	32.5%	60.5%
NDP	3.4%	3.5%
RHINO	—	2.6%
PN	2.2%	—
IND	1.0%	.9%
TOTAL	31,422	29,482

CONSTITUENCY RESULTS	1984	1980
GATINEAU	1984	1980
PC	50.9%	7.0%
LIB	34.4%	78.6%
NDP	12.9%	10.6%
PN	1.5%	—
SC	—	2.2%
RHINO	—	1.4%
COMMONWEALTH	.3%	—
M-L	—	.2%
TOTAL	50,820	45,069
HULL-AYLMER	1984	1980
PC	37.0%	5.3%
LIB	40.6%	68.1%
NDP	19.6%	24.5%
PN	2.4%	—
RHINO	—	1.5%
COMMONWEALTH	.4%	—
NO AFFILIATION	—	.4%
M-L	—	.2%
TOTAL	42,039	41,006
JOLIETTE	1984	1980
PC	73.9%	47.0%
LIB	17.1%	46.1%
NDP	4.2%	4.9%
RHINO	2.9%	—
SC	.4%	1.6%
PN	1.2%	—
COMM	.2%	—
COMMONWEALTH	.1%	—
M-L	—	.4%
TOTAL	52,547	47,441
JONQUIERE	1984	1980
PC	49.6%	3.8%
LIB	38.4%	75.0%
NDP	5.1%	15.0%
PN	4.4%	—
SC	—	4.4%
RHINO	2.5%	—
UP	—	1.3%
M-L	—	.4%
TOTAL	36,700	29,594
KAMOURASKA-RIVIERE-DU-LOUP	1984	1980
PC	53.2%	4.4%
LIB	35.0%	54.8%
NDP	4.2%	—
SC	—	37.6%
RHINO	5.4%	1.0%
RHINO	—	1.0%
PN	1.6%	—
UP	—	1.2%
NO AFFILIATION	.6%	—
TOTAL	36,929	34,858
LABELLE	1984	1980
PC	55.6%	22.2%

CONSTITUENCY RESULTS	1984	1980
LIB	28.4%	66.6%
NDP	9.2%	6.5%
RHINO	3.1%	1.5%
PN	3.0%	—
RHINO	—	1.3%
RHINO	—	.8%
SC	.5%	—
NO AFFILIATION	—	.5%
UP	—	.5%
COMMONWEALTH	.2%	—
M-L	—	.2%
TOTAL	50,892	44,312
LAC-SAINT-JEAN	1984	1980
PC	61.8%	13.7%
LIB	31.0%	63.4%
NDP	5.2%	10.3%
SC	—	8.4%
RHINO	—	3.5%
PN	2.0%	—
UP	—	.8%
TOTAL	40,898	33,572
LANGELIER	1984	1980
PC	43.1%	7.5%
LIB	35.8%	71.5%
NDP	11.7%	8.1%
RHINO	6.6%	8.1%
SC	.5%	3.5%
PN	2.4%	—
UP	—	.7%
M-L	—	.3%
COMM	—	.2%
TOTAL	39,157	34,570
LAPRAIRIE	1984	1980
PC	41.6%	9.7%
LIB	39.6%	72.1%
NDP	13.5%	11.5%
RHINO	2.9%	3.7%
PN	2.2%	—
SC	—	1.9%
LIBERT	—	.6%
UP	—	.4%
COMMONWEALTH	.3%	—
M-L	—	.2%
TOTAL	63,671	51,118
LEVIS	1984	1980
PC	49.6%	8.9%
LIB	26.5%	66.7%
NDP	18.5%	12.1%
SC	.3%	6.4%
RHINO	2.5%	5.0%
PN	2.5%	—
UP	—	.5%
M-L	—	.2%
NO AFFILIATION	—	.2%
TOTAL	65,192	53,257

CONSTITUENCY RESULTS	1984	1980
LONGUEUIL	1984	1980
PC	47.7%	7.1%
LIB	32.4%	69.0%
NDP	10.6%	12.9%
RHINO	4.2%	5.5%
PN	5.0%	—
SC	—	3.6%
UP	—	.8%
COMMONWEALTH	.1%	—
NO AFFILIATION	—	.4%
IND	—	.3%
M-L	—	.2%
COMM	—	.2%
TOTAL	60,661	47,496
LOTBINIERE	1984	1980
PC	48.5%	21.8%
LIB	43.4%	59.1%
NDP	4.2%	7.3%
SC	—	8.8%
HINO	2.0%	2.3%
PN	1.9%	—
NO AFFILIATION	—	.5%
UP	—	.2%
M-L	—	.1%
TOTAL	46,539	41,925
LOUIS-HEBERT	1984	1980
PC	46.0%	10.4%
LIB	35.3%	64.8%
NDP	11.8%	14.0%
RHINO	3.1%	7.2%
SC	.3%	2.4%
IND	1.8%	
PN	1.7%	—
UP	—	1.1%
M-L	—	.2%
TOTAL	64,006	52,863
MANICOUAGAN	1984	1980
PC	71.6%	15.5%
LIB	24.5%	68.7%
NDP	2.4%	6.7%
SC	—	3.8%
RHINO	—	2.7%
RHINO	—	2.3%
PN	1.4%	—
M-L	—	.4%
COMMONWEALTH	.3%	—
TOTAL	39,424	31,319
MATAPEDIA-MATANE	1984	1980
PC	52.7%	11.4%
LIB	32.7%	77.8%
NDP	3.0%	3.3%
PN	11.6%	—
SC	—	4.2%
RHINO	—	3.3%
TOTAL	30,355	27,128

CONSTITUENCY RESULTS	1984	1980
MEGANTIC-COMPTON-STANSTEAD	1984	1980
PC	60.0%	27.4%
LIB	30.6%	57.2%
NDP	6.3%	4.7%
SC	.9%	8.0%
GREEN	1.1%	—
PN	1.0%	—
RHINO	—	2.7%
COMMONWEALTH	.1%	—
TOTAL	42,823	37,692
MONTMORENCY-ORLEANS	1984	1980
PC	47.0%	10.8%
LIB	39.7%	70.1%
NDP	8.1%	7.5%
RHINO	3.3%	4.7%
SC	.6%	4.3%
PN	1.2%	—
IND	—	1.4%
UP	—	.8%
M-L	—	.4%
TOTAL	48,383	40,510
PONTIAC-GATINEAU-LABELLE	1984	1980
PC	62.0%	16.8%
LIB	28.6%	70.4%
NDP	7.6%	9.2%
PN	1.5%	—
RHINO	—	2.1%
UP	—	1.0%
COMMONWEALTH	.4%	—
M-L	—	.6%
TOTAL	35,111	30,694
PORTNEUF	1984	1980
PC	51.1%	7.3%
LIB	38.0%	73.9%
NDP	6.5%	8.3%
SC	.5%	5.9%
RHINO	2.6%	4.1%
PN	1.4%	—
UP	—	.5%
TOTAL	46,604	39,582
QUEBEC-EST	1984	1980
PC	48.1%	6.8%
LIB	34.9%	73.0%
NDP	10.2%	8.8%
RHINO	4.1%	4.9%
SC	.6%	5.3%
PN	1.9%	—
UP	—	.5%
NO AFFILIATION	—	.3%
M-L	—	.3%
COMMONWEALTH	.2%	—
TOTAL	41,111	37,728

CONSTITUENCY RESULTS	1984	1980
RICHELIEU	1984	1980
PC	59.2%	19.9%
LIB	30.8%	68.2%
NDP	4.5%	7.3%
RHINO	2.0%	3.0%
PN	3.0%	—
SC	.4%	—
COMMONWEALTH	.2%	—
NO AFFILIATION	—	.7%
UP	—	.7%
M-L	—	.3%
TOTAL	48,540	40,917
RICHMOND-WOLFE	1984	1980
PC	39.4%	25.2%
LIB	51.4%	63.7%
NDP	4.7%	4.5%
PN	3.8%	—
SC	.8%	4.0%
RHINO	—	2.6%
TOTAL	35,154	33,144
RIMOUSKI-TEMISCOUTA	1984	1980
PC	59.8%	10.4%
LIB	33.4%	56.0%
NDP	2.9%	3.0%
RHINO	1.8%	1.6%
SC	—	28.3%
PN	2.0%	—
COMMONWEALTH	.2%	—
NO AFFILIATION	—	.4%
M-L	—	.2%
TOTAL	42,656	38,342
ROBERVAL	1984	1980
PC	61.9%	1.5%
LIB	34.8%	51.9%
NDP	2.3%	1.7%
PN	1.1%	—
SC	—	43.5%
RHINO	—	1.5%
TOTAL	37,157	34,135
SAINT-HYACINTHE-BAGOT	1984	1980
PC	47.4%	23.9%
LIB	44.1%	67.0%
NDP	4.5%	5.4%
RHINO	2.1%	2.1%
PN	1.9%	—
COMMONWEALTH	.1%	—
IND	—	1.3%
UP	—	.3%
M-L	—	.2%
TOTAL	48,545	42,008
SAINT-JEAN	1984	1980
PC	59.8%	10.6%
LIB	28.8%	72.1%
NDP	7.1%	12.4%

CONSTITUENCY RESULTS	1984	1980
RHINO	2.4%	2.4%
PN	2.0%	—
COMMONWEALTH	.1%	—
SC	—	2.2%
M-L	—	.3%
TOTAL	51,490	41,785

SAINT-MAURICE	1984	1980
PC	35.4%	7.1%
LIB	58.9%	76.7%
NDP	3.5%	5.5%
PN	2.2%	—
SC	—	6.6%
RHINO	—	3.4%
UP	—	.5%
M-L	—	.3%
TOTAL	40,843	35,666

SHEFFORD	1984	1980
PC	42.9%	20.8%
LIB	47.5%	68.5%
NDP	6.7%	7.8%
PN	2.9%	—
RHINO	—	2.7%
M-L	—	.3%
TOTAL	53,632	47,390

SHERBROOKE	1984	1980
PC	51.5%	9.3%
LIB	33.8%	71.8%
NDP	9.8%	10.0%
RHINO	2.4%	2.4%
RHINO	—	1.3%
PN	1.6%	—
SC	.5%	4.2%
COMMONWEALTH	.2%	—
COMM	.2%	.2%
IND	—	.5%
UP	—	.2%
M-L	—	.2%
TOTAL	43,171	37,922

TEMISCAMINGUE	1984	1980
PC	50.2%	5.2%
LIB	34.0%	61.0%
NDP	5.4%	4.4%
PN	5.3%	—
RHINO	3.6%	3.3%
SC	1.6%	24.0%
UP	—	1.4%
NO AFFILIATION	—	.4%
M-L	—	.3%
TOTAL	40,501	36,104

TERREBONNE	1984	1980
PC	60.3%	9.1%
LIB	26.2%	68.4%
NDP	8.9%	12.9%
RHINO	—	3.5%

CONSTITUENCY RESULTS	1984	1980
PN	4.2%	—
COMMONWEALTH	.4%	—
SC	—	5.4%
UP	—	.4%
M-L	—	.3%
TOTAL	72,668	52,760

TROIS-RIVIERES	1984	1980
PC	63.9%	12.9%
LIB	24.3%	68.5%
NDP	4.6%	11.1%
PN	4.4%	—
RHINO	2.4%	—
NO AFFILIATION	—	5.5%
NO AFFILIATION	—	.8%
UP	—	.7%
M-L	—	.5%
COMM	.3%	—
TOTAL	41,982	34,741

VERCHERES	1984	1980
PC	56.0%	10.3%
LIB	28.0%	68.1%
NDP	9.5%	12.8%
RHINO	3.2%	5.1%
PN	3.1%	—
COMMONWEALTH	.2%	—
SC	—	2.8%
UP	—	.8%
M-L	—	.2%
TOTAL	69,067	54,877

ISLAND OF MONTREAL AND ILE JESUS BOURASSA	1984	1980
PC	40.6%	7.9%
LIB	44.0%	76.5%
NDP	8.1%	12.7%
RHINO	3.5%	—
PN	2.5%	—
UP	—	2.2%
M-L	—	.8%
SC	.5%	—
COMMONWEALTH	.3%	—
NO AFFILIATION	.2%	—
NO AFFILIATION	.2%	—
TOTAL	46,017	40,430

DOLLARD	1984	1980
PC	45.9%	10.7%
LIB	37.7%	76.5%
NDP	11.6%	11.7%
RHINO	2.2%	—
PN	1.7%	—
UP	—	0.6%
LIBERT	.7%	.3%
COMMONWEALTH	.2%	—
M-L	—	.3%
TOTAL	56,856	49,523

CONSTITUENCY RESULTS	1984	1980
DUVERNAY	1984	1980
PC	50.4%	7.6%
LIB	31.1%	72.4%
NDP	8.5%	10.6%
PN	5.4%	—
RHINO	3.5%	5.2%
IND	0.8%	—
SC	.3%	3.2%
COMMONWEALTH	.1%	—
UP	—	.5%
M-L	—	.2%
COMM	—	.2%
TOTAL	59,331	47,715
GAMELIN	1984	1980
PC	44.5%	8.0%
LIB	37.3%	72.4%
NDP	10.1%	11.2%
RHINO	3.5%	4.1%
PN	2.8%	—
SC	—	2.9%
GREEN	1.5%	—
NO AFFILIATION	—	.5%
NO AFFILIATION	—	.3%
COMMONWEALTH	.2%	—
UP	—	.5%
M-L	—	.2%
TOTAL	46,879	40,379
HOCHELAGA-MAISONNEUVE	1984	1980
PC	41.2%	6.9%
LIB	38.0%	73.4%
NDP	11.2%	9.5%
RHINO	5.8%	4.9%
PN	3.4%	—
SC	—	3.0%
NO AFFILIATION	—	1.0%
IND	—	.7%
COMM	.3%	—
M-L	—	.3%
UP	—	.3%
COMMONWEALTH	.2%	—
TOTAL	32,139	28,814
LACHINE	1984	1980
PC	51.7%	30.1%
LIB	32.2%	59.7%
NDP	12.0%	8.2%
RHINO	2.1%	1.6%
PN	1.1%	—
LIBERT	.5%	.3%
IND	.3%	—
IND	.2%	—
M-L	—	.1%
TOTAL	47,049	42,689
LASALLE	1984	1980
PC	46.7%	7.5%
LIB	39.1%	78.2%

CONSTITUENCY RESULTS	1984	1980
NDP	9.6%	12.4%
RHINO	2.7%	—
PN	1.7%	—
UP	—	1.2%
M-L	—	.6%
COMMONWEALTH	.3%	—
TOTAL	49,725	41,624
LAURIER	1984	1980
PC	28.7%	6.5%
LIB	34.6%	66.7%
NDP	17.1%	9.1%
RHINO	12.1%	12.6%
PN	3.4%	—
SC	.7%	2.2%
GREEN	2.8%	—
NO AFFILIATION	—	1.4%
COMM	.5%	.4%
IND	—	.4%
UP	—	.4%
M-L	—	.3%
COMMONWEALTH	.2%	—
TOTAL	26,898	24,303
LAVAL	1984	1980
PC	47.6%	7.3%
LIB	35.7%	75.3%
NDP	12.7%	11.2%
PN	3.6%	—
RHINO	—	3.3%
SC	—	2.2%
COMMONWEALTH	.5%	—
UP	—	.5%
M-L	—	.3%
TOTAL	64,486	51,206
LAVAL-DES-RAPIDES	1984	1980
PC	39.3%	6.9%
LIB	43.9%	75.0%
NDP	10.1%	10.6%
RHINO	3.7%	4.8%
PN	2.9%	—
SC	—	2.1%
UP	—	.5%
COMMONWEALTH	.2%	—
M-L	—	.2%
TOTAL	51,916	44,444
MONTREAL-MERCIER	1984	1980
PC	46.4%	8.1%
LIB	35.8%	70.6%
NDP	9.1%	11.0%
SC	—	4.9%
RHINO	3.8%	4.7%
PN	4.7%	—
UP	—	.4%
M-L	—	.4%
COMMONWEALTH	.3%	—
TOTAL	54,080	38,880

CONSTITUENCY RESULTS	1984	1980
MONTREAL-SAINTE-MARIE	1984	1980
PC	34.7%	12.8%
LIB	43.4%	68.5%
NDP	11.2%	8.7%
RHINO	7.4%	5.9%
PN	3.1%	—
SC	—	2.2%
NO AFFILIATION	—	1.1%
M-L	—	.4%
UP	—	.4%
COMMONWEALTH	.2%	—
TOTAL	31,509	27,973
MOUNT ROYAL	1984	1980
PC	39.1%	10.6%
LIB	47.5%	81.2%
NDP	9.9%	5.7%
RHINO	1.6%	1.7%
PN	.8%	—
LIBERT	.7%	.3%
IND	.2%	.4%
M-L	—	.2%
COMMONWEALTH	.2%	—
TOTAL	47,854	41,637
NOTRE DAME DE GRACE-LACHINE EAST	1984	1980
PC	38.4%	14.7%
LIB	43.4%	71.2%
NDP	14.0%	11.6%
RHINO	2.4%	2.3%
PN	1.4%	—
COMMONWEALTH	.3%	—
M-L	—	.3%
TOTAL	41,238	38,792
OUTREMONT	1984	1980
PC	29.3%	7.3%
LIB	40.9%	71.5%
NDP	18.9%	12.4%
RHINO	4.2%	6.4%
PN	3.3%	—
GREEN	2.5%	—
NO AFFILIATION	—	.9%
COMM	.5%	.5%
COMMONWEALTH	.4%	—
UP	—	.4%
IND	—	.4%
M-L	—	.2%
TOTAL	35,458	32,179
PAPINEAU	1984	1980
PC	36.9%	5.5%
LIB	39.0%	74.7%
NDP	13.1%	9.3%
RHINO	5.9%	5.4%
PN	3.6%	—
SC	.5%	3.3%

CONSTITUENCY RESULTS	1984	1980
NO AFFILIATION	.3%	.8%
UP	—	.6%
COMM	.5%	.2%
COMMONWEALTH	.4%	—
M-L	—	.2%
TOTAL	32,707	29,990
ROSEMONT	1984	1980
PC	42.2%	6.5%
LIB	38.7%	75.9%
NDP	10.9%	9.5%
RHINO	4.3%	3.7%
PN	2.7%	—
SC	.4%	2.6%
NO AFFILIATION	.3%	.6%
IND	—	.6%
UP	—	.4%
COMM	.4%	—
M-L	—	.3%
COMMONWEALTH	.2%	—
TOTAL	37,377	34,989
SAINT-DENIS	1984	1980
PC	31.3%	6.3%
LIB	48.4%	77.4%
NDP	11.8%	9.5%
RHINO	4.1%	3.4%
SC	—	2.0%
PN	2.5%	—
IND	.8%	—
COMM	.7%	.5%
COMMONWEALTH	.3%	—
UP	—	.4%
M-L	—	.5%
TOTAL	38,710	36,663
SAINT-HENRI-WESTMOUNT	1984	1980
PC	35.2%	18.1%
LIB	45.3%	67.5%
NDP	14.6%	10.2%
RHINO	3.2%	3.1%
PN	1.6%	—
LIBERT	—	.5%
M-L	—	.3%
NO AFFILIATION	—	.3%
COMMONWEALTH	.1%	—
TOTAL	40,281	36,905
SAINT-JACQUES	1984	1980
PC	37.5%	12.2%
LIB	39.6%	71.2%
NDP	14.8%	9.4%
RHINO	4.4%	4.3%
PN	2.7%	—
NO AFFILIATION	—	.9%
COMM	.6%	.4%
LIBERT	—	.6%
UP	—	.5%
COMMONWEALTH	.4%	—

CONSTITUENCY RESULTS	1984	1980
M-L	—	.4%
NO AFFILIATION	—	.2%
TOTAL	27,433	24,934

SAINT-LEONARD-ANJOU	1984	1980
PC	39.3%	5.7%
LIB	41.4%	81.1%
NDP	12.7%	7.2%
RHINO	3.6%	3.0%
PN	2.8%	—
SC	—	2.3%
UP	—	.5%
M-L	—	.2%
COMMONWEALTH	.2%	—
TOTAL	59,232	52,055

SAINT-MICHEL-AHUNTSIC	1984	1980
PC	38.0%	5.7%
LIB	42.5%	75.5%
NDP	12.0%	9.5%
RHINO	3.8%	4.5%
PN	3.1%	—
SC	—	3.0%
UP	—	.8%
COMM	.5%	.3%
NO AFFILIATION	—	.5%
M-L	—	.3%
COMMONWEALTH	.2%	—
TOTAL	40,652	36,050

VAUDREUIL	1984	1980
PC	54.5%	11.6%
LIB	29.6%	72.6%
NDP	11.6%	13.5%
RHINO	2.1%	—
PN	1.5%	—
UP	—	1.0%
LIBERT	.5%	.9%
M-L	—	.4%
COMMONWEALTH	.2%	—
TOTAL	68,825	53,971

VERDUN-SAINT-PAUL	1984	1980
PC	43.5%	9.4%
LIB	41.2%	75.3%
NDP	9.8%	9.9%
RHINO	3.3%	3.1%
PN	2.0%	—
SC	—	1.6%
UP	—	.4%
M-L	—	.2%
COMMONWEALTH	.3%	—
TOTAL	39,927	36,608

NOVA SCOTIA ANNAPOLIS VALLEY-HANTS	1984	1980
PC	53.9%	42.0%

CONSTITUENCY RESULTS	1984	1980
LIB	28.5%	31.3%
NDP	16.0%	25.3%
RHINO	1.7%	.8%
IND	—	.6%
TOTAL	43,792	40,870

CAPE BRETON-EAST RICHMOND	1984	1980
PC	32.8%	22.4%
LIB	55.8%	39.3%
NDP	10.2%	38.3%
RHINO	1.2%	—
TOTAL	36,319	31,777

CAPE BRETON HIGHLANDS-CANSO	1984	1980
PC	50.1%	35.3%
LIB	38.8%	50.4%
NDP	11.1%	13.5%
IND	—	.8%
TOTAL	38,705	36,235

CAPE BRETON-THE SYDNEYS	1984	1980
PC	37.5%	26.6%
LIB	44.1%	43.8%
NDP	18.3%	29.4%
M-L	—	.3%
TOTAL	36,382	34,620

CENTRAL NOVA	1984	1980
PC	61.0%	48.0%
LIB	26.0%	34.3%
NDP	13.0%	17.7%
TOTAL	35,182	32,430

CUMBERLAND-COLCHESTER	1984	1980
PC	57.3%	46.3%
LIB	29.6%	34.5%
NDP	13.1%	17.9%
IND	—	.9%
IND	—	.5%
TOTAL	42,196	39,842

DARTMOUTH-HALIFAX EAST	1984	1980
PC	55.0%	41.9%
LIB	26.1%	37.7%
NDP	19.0%	20.4%
TOTAL	50,136	42,932

HALIFAX	1984	1980
PC	44.8%	38.6%
LIB	34.4%	41.6%
NDP	20.5%	19.7%
NO AFFILIATION	.4%	—
M-L	—	.1%
TOTAL	41,940	40,716

CONSTITUENCY RESULTS	1984	1980
HALIFAX WEST	1984	1980
PC	54.3%	40.0%
LIB	24.3%	38.6%
NDP	20.8%	20.9%
IND	.6%	.6%
TOTAL	55,797	48,026
SOUTH SHORE	1984	1980
PC	56.7%	44.4%
LIB	29.0%	38.3%
NDP	14.3%	16.1%
RHINO	—	1.2%
TOTAL	39,419	36,354
SOUTH WEST NOVA	1984	1980
PC	50.6%	36.8%
LIB	41.9%	49.8%
NDP	7.6%	12.8%
IND	—	.6%
TOTAL	40,724	38,440
NEW BRUNSWICK CARLETON-CHARLOTTE	1984	1980
PC	61.6%	47.4%
LIB	24.1%	36.1%
NDP	14.3%	15.2%
NO AFFILIATION	—	1.3%
TOTAL	32,224	30,743
FUNDY-ROYAL	1984	1980
PC	56.6%	40.8%
LIB	25.0%	36.9%
NDP	18.5%	21.1%
NO AFFILIATION	—	.8%
NO AFFILIATION	—	.4%
TOTAL	45,990	41,150
GLOUCESTER	1984	1980
PC	55.1%	19.6%
LIB	38.4%	63.7%
NDP	5.1%	12.8%
RHINO	—	2.1%
RHINO	—	1.0%
IND	1.4%	—
NO AFFILIATION	—	.6%
M-L	—	.2%
TOTAL	42,674	34,913
MADAWASKA-VICTORIA	1984	1980
PC	51.9%	22.9%
LIB	41.9%	65.8%
NDP	6.2%	11.3%
TOTAL	31,624	26,112
MONCTON	1984	1980
PC	57.2%	34.9%
LIB	27.8%	48.0%
NDP	14.6%	16.7%

CONSTITUENCY RESULTS	1984	1980
IND	.5%	—
NO AFFILIATION	—	.3%
M-L	—	.1%
TOTAL	52,365	46,630
NORTHUMBER-LAND-MIRAMICHI	1984	1980
PC	53.9%	27.8%
LIB	37.7%	54.8%
NDP	8.4%	17.4%
TOTAL	31,765	27,010
RESTIGOUCHE	1984	1980
PC	45.7%	18.9%
LIB	39.7%	61.3%
NDP	14.7%	16.5%
RHINO	—	2.6%
NO AFFILIATION	—	.8%
TOTAL	30,865	27,035
SAINT JOHN	1984	1980
PC	52.2%	39.0%
LIB	25.5%	41.4%
NDP	21.2%	18.9%
LIBERT	.8%	.2%
SC	.3%	—
IND	—	.3%
M-L	—	.1%
TOTAL	31,809	31,667
WESTMORLAND-KENT	1984	1980
PC	38.0%	16.6%
LIB	41.8%	67.1%
NDP	20.3%	16.3%
TOTAL	35,228	32,219
YORK-SUNBURY	1984	1980
PC	58.9%	47.7%
LIB	23.1%	37.0%
NDP	17.2%	14.6%
IND	.9%	.5%
LIBERT	—	.3%
TOTAL	42,806	38,251
MANITOBA BRANDON-SOURIS	1984	1980
PC	52.2%	46.9%
LIB	14.6%	28.1%
NDP	15.6%	24.8%
CONFED RWP	17.5%	—
M-L	—	.2%
TOTAL	36,044	34,344
CHURCHILL	1984	1980
PC	33.7%	25.5%
LIB	18.0%	29.7%
NDP	45.6%	43.3%
IND	1.6%	—
RHINO	—	1.5%

CONSTITUENCY RESULTS	1984	1980
LIBERT	1.2%	—
TOTAL	23,769	23,847

DAUPHIN-SWAN RIVER	1984	1980
PC	42.6%	38.4%
LIB	15.5%	16.8%
NDP	36.3%	44.8%
CONFED RWP	5.7%	—
TOTAL	28,133	28,925

LISGAR	1984	1980
PC	49.5%	62.7%
LIB	14.1%	24.3%
NDP	6.5%	11.6%
CONFED RWP	28.6%	—
RHINO	1.4%	—
NO AFFILIATION	—	1.4%
TOTAL	31,445	28,822

PORTAGE-MARQUETTE	1984	1980
PC	49.4%	53.0%
LIB	13.4%	22.8%
NDP	14.3%	23.6%
CONFED RWP	22.3%	—
LIBERT	.7%	—
M-L	—	.6%
TOTAL	31,147	30,587

PROVENCHER	1984	1980
PC	58.3%	44.9%
LIB	14.1%	25.3%
NDP	20.1%	28.4%
CONFED RWP	6.8%	—
RHINO	—	1.3%
LIBERT	.7%	—
TOTAL	34,462	32,662

ST. BONIFACE	1984	1980
PC	39.7%	29.4%
LIB	34.0%	45.3%
NDP	22.9%	25.2%
CONFED RWP	3.4%	—
M-L	—	.1%
TOTAL	49,239	44,368

SELKIRK-INTERLAKE	1984	1980
PC	40.7%	36.0%
LIB	10.4%	18.1%
NDP	38.7%	45.7%
CONFED RWP	9.8%	—
LIBERT	.5%	—
M-L	—	.3%
TOTAL	33,812	32,952

WINNIPEG-ASSINIBOINE	1984	1980
PC	52.4%	49.1%

CONSTITUENCY RESULTS	1984	1980
LIB	30.8%	34.2%
NDP	13.4%	16.2%
CONFED RWP	2.6%	—
LIBERT	.9%	—
IND	—	.5%
M-L	—	.1%
TOTAL	52,650	45,134

WINNIPEG-BIRDS HILL	1984	1980
PC	39.6%	29.4%
LIB	10.4%	15.4%
NDP	45.8%	54.3%
CONFED RWP	2.1%	—
RHINO	1.1%	.7%
IND	1.1%	—
M-L	—	.1%
TOTAL	52,181	45,459

WINNIPEG-FORT GARRY	1984	1980
PC	40.7%	34.4%
LIB	45.7%	46.4%
NDP	12.7%	18.1%
RHINO	—	1.0%
LIBERT	.7%	—
COMM	.3%	—
M-L	—	.2%
TOTAL	46,573	40,336

WINNIPEG NORTH	1984	1980
PC	30.2%	22.6%
LIB	24.8%	25.9%
NDP	43.3%	50.5%
COMM	.7%	.5%
IND	.6%	—
IND	.4%	—
M-L	—	.4%
TOTAL	42,041	36,735

WINNIPEG NORTH CENTRE	1984	1980
PC	28.3%	18.6%
LIB	22.5%	23.4%
NDP	46.1%	57.0%
IND	2.1%	—
IND	1.0%	—
COMM	—	.8%
M-L	—	.3%
TOTAL	22,891	22,171

WINNIPEG-ST. JAMES	1984	1980
PC	42.5%	36.0%
LIB	20.4%	25.5%
NDP	33.4%	37.5%
CONFED RWP	2.8%	—
RHINO	—	.8%
LIBERT	.6%	—
COMM	.3%	—

CONSTITUENCY RESULTS	1984	1980
M-L	—	.3%
TOTAL	29,453	29,562

BRITISH COLUMBIA

BURNABY	1984	1980
PC	35.1%	36.6%
LIB	16.3%	20.8%
NDP	48.0%	42.4%
GREEN	.6%	—
M-L	—	.2%
TOTAL	58,991	50,872

CAPILANO	1984	1980
PC	56.5%	59.4%
LIB	26.8%	24.5%
NDP	12.5%	14.6%
RHINO	1.2%	1.6%
GREEN	1.5%	—
IND	1.3%	—
LIBERT	.4%	—
TOTAL	50,694	44,353

CARIBOO-CHILCOTIN	1984	1980
PC	54.5%	40.8%
LIB	13.0%	25.0%
NDP	30.6%	34.0%
GREEN	1.0%	—
SC	.9%	—
M-L	—	.3%
TOTAL	37,705	30,316

COMOX-POWELL RIVER	1984	1980
PC	43.4%	32.4%
LIB	9.5%	18.1%
NDP	44.6%	49.0%
GREEN	.9%	—
CONFED RWP	.7%	—
SC	.6%	—
COMM	.4%	.6%
TOTAL	61,173	51,065

COWICHAN-MALAHAT-THE ISLANDS	1984	1980
PC	42.1%	39.5%
LIB	10.8%	11.2%
NDP	45.1%	48.2%
RHINO	—	1.0%
GREEN	.7%	—
LIBERT	.6%	—
CONFED RWP	.5%	—
COMM	—	.2%
IND	.1%	—
IND	.1%	—
TOTAL	54,498	45,997

ESQUIMALT-SAANICH	1984	1980
PC	48.3%	45.0%

CONSTITUENCY RESULTS	1984	1980
LIB	14.5%	18.1%
NDP	35.1%	34.5%
IND	—	1.4%
RHINO	—	1.0%
GREEN	.8%	—
CONFED RWP	.5%	—
SC	.5%	—
LIBERT	.3%	—
COMM	.1%	—
TOTAL	65,790	55,443

FRASER VALLEY EAST	1984	1980
PC	59.9%	49.7%
LIB	14.8%	21.5%
NDP	23.9%	24.2%
IND	—	4.7%
LIBERT	1.4%	—
TOTAL	53,529	44,231

FRASER VALLEY WEST	1984	1980
PC	54.7%	50.6%
LIB	12.7%	16.7%
NDP	30.2%	32.6%
RHINO	.7%	—
LIBERT	.6%	—
GREEN	.4%	—
CONFED RWP	.3%	—
COMM	.2%	—
M-L	—	.2%
NO AFFILIATION	.1%	—
TOTAL	65,759	50,904

KAMLOOPS-SHUSWAP	1984	1980
PC	36.3%	35.1%
LIB	8.3%	25.3%
NDP	54.1%	39.1%
RHINO	.6%	.5%
GREEN	.4%	—
CONFED RWP	.2%	—
IND	.1%	—
TOTAL	56,423	45,767

KOOTENAY EAST-REVELSTOKE	1984	1980
PC	46.5%	38.0%
LIB	11.5%	22.1%
NDP	40.8%	39.9%
IND	1.2%	-
TOTAL	38,993	33,353

KOOTENAY WEST	1984	1980
PC	47.4%	40.2%
LIB	7.4%	16.8%
NDP	45.2%	43.0%
TOTAL	33,324	28,418

CONSTITUENCY RESULTS	1984	1980
MISSION-PORT MOODY	1984	1980
PC	47.5%	36.0%
LIB	11.0%	15.8%
NDP	40.2%	47.2%
GREEN	.8%	—
SC	.5%	.7%
COMM	—	.3%
TOTAL	64,541	49,209
NANAIMO-ALBERNI	1984	1980
PC	45.8%	34.8%
LIB	9.9%	14.3%
NDP	42.9%	49.2%
RHINO	—	1.2%
GREEN	.9%	—
COMM	.4%	.4%
NO AFFILIATION	.1%	—
M-L	—	.1%
TOTAL	59,834	48,949
NEW WESTMINSTER-COQUITLAM	1984	1980
PC	40.0%	34.1%
LIB	12.7%	19.1%
NDP	46.2%	46.4%
RHINO	.9%	—
COMM	.3%	.4%
TOTAL	45,769	42,007
NORTH VANCOUVER-BURNABY	1984	1980
PC	43.6%	38.1%
LIB	28.7%	34.8%
NDP	25.7%	26.9%
RHINO	.8%	—
GREEN	.4%	—
LIBERT	.4%	—
COMM	.2%	—
NO AFFILIATION	.1%	—
CONFED RWP	.1%	—
SC	—	.2%
M-L	—	.1%
TOTAL	49,855	44,027
OKANAGAN NORTH	1984	1980
PC	56.1%	48.7%
LIB	15.5%	22.2%
NDP	26.8%	29.1%
SC	1.6%	—
TOTAL	64,032	51,295
OKANAGAN-SIMILKAMEEN	1984	1980
PC	52.2%	45.0%
LIB	15.6%	22.1%
NDP	29.3%	30.7%
SC	.8%	1.4%

CONSTITUENCY RESULTS	1984	1980
CONFED RWP	1.3%	—
GREEN	.8%	—
RHINO	—	.7%
TOTAL	51,849	42,562
PRINCE GEORGE-BULKLEY VALLEY	1984	1980
PC	49.3%	39.5%
LIB	13.4%	28.6%
NDP	34.6%	31.9%
LIBERT	1.3%	—
RHINO	1.1%	—
IND	.4%	—
TOTAL	38,339	32,013
PRINCE GEORGE-PEACE RIVER	1984	1980
PC	62.4%	52.1%
LIB	9.9%	19.3%
NDP	24.1%	26.2%
SC	1.0%	2.4%
RHINO	1.1%	—
CONFED RWP	1.0%	—
LIBERT	.4%	—
TOTAL	33,879	26,092
RICHMOND-SOUTH DELTA	1984	1980
PC	55.4%	52.0%
LIB	19.4%	23.4%
NDP	23.8%	24.2%
GREEN	.6%	—
IND	.4%	—
CONFED RWP	.4%	—
COMM	—	.3%
M-L	—	.1%
TOTAL	68,892	56,163
SKEENA	1984	1980
PC	36.2%	23.1%
LIB	16.6%	26.6%
NDP	45.8%	49.5%
RHINO	1.4%	—
NO AFFILIATION	—	.8%
TOTAL	30,956	26,817
SURREY-WHITE ROCK-NORTH DELTA	1984	1980
PC	53.6%	48.9%
LIB	14.6%	17.0%
NDP	30.6%	33.1%
RHINO	.7%	.8%
GREEN	.4%	—
COMM	.2%	.1%
M-L	—	.1%
TOTAL	73,797	57,548
VANCOUVER CENTRE	1984	1980
PC	43.2%	35.3%

CONSTITUENCY RESULTS	1984	1980
LIB	21.2%	31.4%
NDP	32.4%	31.8%
GREEN	1.1%	—
RHINO	1.0%	.7%
LIBERT	.6%	—
COMM	.3%	.4%
CONFED RWP	.2%	—
IND	—	.1%
M-L	—	.1%
TOTAL	50,210	46,675

VANCOUVER EAST	1984	1980
PC	20.2%	14.6%
LIB	25.4%	40.0%
NDP	51.8%	43.9%
RHINO	1.0%	.6%
LIBERT	.9%	—
COMM	.7%	.6%
NO AFFILIATION	—	.2%
M-L	—	.1%
TOTAL	35,649	32,438

VANCOUVER KINGSWAY	1984	1980
PC	18.1%	21.9%
LIB	29.5%	30.3%
NDP	51.1%	46.9%
GREEN	.8%	—
COMM	.5%	.4%
IND	—	.3%
M-L	—	.2%
TOTAL	39,490	36,131

VANCOUVER QUADRA	1984	1980
PC	37.5%	46.1%
LIB	43.9%	30.7%
NDP	16.8%	21.8%
RHINO	.4%	.9%
GREEN	.8%	—
COMM	0.0%	—
IND	.2%	.2%
SC	—	.2%
IND	0.0%	.1%
IND	0.0%	—
LIBERT	.2%	—
NO AFFILIATION	.1%	.1%
M-L	—	.1%
COMMONWEALTH	0%	—
TOTAL	49,604	45,545

VANCOUVER-SOUTH	1984	1980
PC	54.9%	53.3%
LIB	20.5%	24.5%
NDP	23.5%	21.3%
GREEN	1.1%	—
RHINO	—	.8%
M-L	—	.2%
TOTAL	46,414	41,828

CONSTITUENCY RESULTS	1984	1980
VICTORIA	1984	1980
PC	46.3%	50.3%
LIB	12.6%	14.4%
NDP	38.6%	34.3%
GREEN	1.1%	—
RHINO	.5%	.9%
LIBERT	.4%	—
CONFED RWP	.3%	—
IND	.2%	—
M-L	—	.1%
TOTAL	53,060	49,794

PRINCE EDWARD ISLAND CARDIGAN	1984	1980
PC	53.4%	44.9%
LIB	42.1%	48.2%
NDP	4.5%	5.9%
IND	—	1.0%
TOTAL	19,801	17,830

EGMONT	1984	1980
PC	44.6%	42.6%
LIB	49.8%	52.4%
NDP	5.6%	5.0%
TOTAL	17,630	16,496

HILLSBOROUGH	1984	1980
PC	53.2%	47.7%
LIB	39.3%	43.8%
NDP	4.9%	8.3%
NO AFFILIATION	1.9%	—
IND	.5%	—
GREEN	.2%	—
M-L	—	.2%
TOTAL	17,214	14,956

MALPEQUE	1984	1980
PC	56.4%	50.1%
LIB	33.0%	42.7%
NDP	10.7%	7.2%
TOTAL	18,769	16,923

SASKATCHEWAN ASSINIBOIA	1984	1980
PC	47.2%	35.9%
LIB	19.1%	32.5%
NDP	32.0%	31.0%
CONFED RWP	1.8%	—
SC	—	.6%
TOTAL	33,946	31,306

HUMBOLDT-LAKE CENTRE	1984	1980
PC	38.0%	36.4%
LIB	17.3%	21.9%
NDP	43.5%	41.6%
CONFED RWP	1.2%	—
TOTAL	34,687	31,815

KINDERSLEY-LLOYDMINSTER	1984	1980
PC	58.3%	46.3%

CONSTITUENCY RESULTS	1984	1980
LIB	11.4%	21.6%
NDP	29.2%	31.2%
CONFED RWP	1.2%	—
RHINO	—	1.0%
TOTAL	35,063	30,734
MACKENZIE	1984	1980
PC	40.0%	41.6%
LIB	17.4%	17.5%
NDP	38.1%	40.2%
CONFED RWP	4.5%	
COMM	—	.6%
TOTAL	28,481	25,942
MOOSE JAW	1984	1980
PC	46.0%	46.4%
LIB	13.9%	18.5%
NDP	38.8%	34.5%
CONFED RWP	1.3%	—
IND	—	.4%
LIBERT	—	.2%
TOTAL	34,349	30,872
PRINCE ALBERT	1984	1980
PC	34.8%	32.5%
LIB	29.0%	32.8%
NDP	35.6%	34.8%
CONFED RWP	.7%	—
TOTAL	37,569	33,339
QU'APPELLE-MOOSE MOUNTAIN	1984	1980
PC	49.8%	49.6%
LIB	16.9%	21.9%
NDP	29.0%	28.5%
CONFED RWP	2.3%	—
IND	2.1%	—
TOTAL	29,039	27,590
REGINA EAST	1984	1980
PC	33.3%	34.1%
LIB	20.9%	27.8%
NDP	44.9%	36.8%
CONFED RWP	.9%	—
RHINO	—	.8%
NO AFFILIATION	—	.2%
M-L	—	.2%
COMM	—	.1%
TOTAL	45,621	37,010
REGINA WEST	1984	1980
PC	31.5%	32.5%
LIB	20.4%	24.8%
NDP	46.8%	42.2%
RHINO	.6%	—
CONFED RWP	.5%	—
NO AFFILIATION	—	.4%
M-L	—	.1%
COMM	.2%	—
TOTAL	50,971	41,123

CONSTITUENCY RESULTS	1984	1980
SASKATOON EAST	1984	1980
PC	36.9%	32.9%
LIB	25.7%	30.5%
NDP	36.0%	34.5%
NO AFFILIATION	—	1.9%
RHINO	.7%	—
GREEN	.4%	—
CONFED RWP	.3%	—
M-L	—	.2%
TOTAL	46,284	37,632
SASKATOON WEST	1984	1980
PC	49.7%	43.3%
LIB	12.1%	19.9%
NDP	36.1%	36.5%
RHINO	1.0%	—
CONFED RWP	.6%	—
GREEN	.3%	—
IND	.2%	—
M-L	—	.2%
TOTAL	52,368	40,701
SWIFT CURRENT-MAPLE CREEK	1984	1980
PC	49.7%	48.0%
LIB	20.3%	21.1%
NDP	27.9%	31.0%
CONFED RWP	2.0%	—
TOTAL	29,335	26,928
THE BATTLEFORDS-MEADOW LAKE	1984	1980
PC	43.3%	34.1%
LIB	13.4%	29.5%
NDP	42.2%	35.8%
CONFED RWP	1.1%	—
IND	—	.7%
TOTAL	29,775	27,428
YORKTON-MELVILLE	1984	1980
PC	33.4%	37.3%
LIB	14.2%	17.0%
NDP	51.3%	45.7%
CONFED RWP	1.1%	—
TOTAL	35,312	33,354
ALBERTA ATHABASCA	1984	1980
PC	68.3%	47.5%
LIB	12.0%	35.1%
NDP	17.1%	15.1%
CONFED RWP	1.7%	—
SC	1.0%	1.7%
IND	—	.7%
TOTAL	35,130	27,986
BOW RIVER	1984	1980
PC	76.2%	76.6%
LIB	7.2%	14.7%

CONSTITUENCY RESULTS	1984	1980
NDP	9.3%	7.1%
RHINO	4.2%	—
CONFED RWP	2.6%	—
SC	.6%	1.7%
TOTAL	56,475	39,771

CALGARY CENTRE	1984	1980
PC	66.4%	57.4%
LIB	15.9%	29.9%
NDP	13.7%	9.2%
RHINO	—	2.4%
GREEN	2.0%	—
CONFED RWP	1.6%	—
SC	—	.8%
LIBERT	.5%	—
COMM	—	.2%
M-L	—	.1%
TOTAL	37,562	32,426

CALGARY EAST	1984	1980
PC	58.9%	52.8%
LIB	23.6%	26.7%
NDP	13.7%	10.3%
NO AFFILIATION	—	7.5%
IND	1.6%	—
RHINO	—	1.5%
CONFED RWP	1.1%	—
SC	.6%	1.0%
LIBERT	.5%	—
COMM	.2%	.1%
M-L	—	.1%
TOTAL	62,572	43,669

CALGARY NORTH	1984	1980
PC	72.8%	63.4%
LIB	12.7%	25.9%
NDP	13.1%	7.7%
RHINO	—	2.1%
IND	1.4%	—
SC	—	.8%
M-L	—	.1%
TOTAL	53,863	41,312

CALGARY SOUTH	1984	1980
PC	77.9%	68.1%
LIB	11.0%	23.0%
NDP	8.6%	5.5%
RHINO	—	1.7%
CONFED RWP	1.2%	—
IND	1.1%	1.0%
COMMONWEALTH	.2%	—
SC	—	.6%
M-L	—	.1%
TOTAL	71,354	51,192

CALGARY WEST	1984	1980
PC	74.7%	65.9%
LIB	11.4%	23.1%
NDP	10.8%	7.7%

CONSTITUENCY RESULTS	1984	1980
RHINO	—	2.5%
GREEN	1.2%	—
CONFED RWP	1.0%	—
SC	.4%	.7%
LIBERT	.5%	—
M-L	—	.1%
TOTAL	50,285	40,451

CROWFOOT	1984	1980
PC	77.8%	76.6%
LIB	7.4%	15.5%
NDP	9.3%	6.2%
CONFED RWP	4.6%	—
SC	.9%	1.6%
TOTAL	33,780	30,662

EDMONTON EAST	1984	1980
PC	48.5%	53.9%
LIB	18.1%	27.6%
NDP	23.1%	17.3%
IND	8.6%	—
GREEN	.7%	—
CONFED RWP	.7%	—
SC	—	.7%
COMM	.4%	.3%
M-L	—	.2%
TOTAL	33,248	27,537

EDMONTON NORTH	1984	1980
PC	57.3%	59.0%
LIB	16.4%	26.7%
NDP	24.3%	14.1%
CONFED RWP	1.0%	—
SC	.7%	—
COMM	.4%	—
M-L	—	.3%
TOTAL	50,749	36,357

EDMONTON SOUTH	1984	1980
PC	62.5%	61.1%
LIB	15.9%	26.2%
NDP	18.1%	11.7%
CONFED RWP	1.1%	—
GREEN	1.0%	—
RHINO	1.0%	—
IND	—	.8%
SC	.5%	—
M-L	—	.2%
TOTAL	52,046	40,672

EDMONTON-STRATHCONA	1984	1980
PC	61.4%	59.4%
LIB	15.5%	27.2%
NDP	20.2%	12.0%
CONFED RWP	1.4%	—
RHINO	—	1.1%
GREEN	.9%	—
SC	.4%	—
COMM	.3%	.3%

CONSTITUENCY RESULTS	1984	1980
M-L	—	.1%
TOTAL	54,877	40,285
EDMONTON WEST	**1984**	**1980**
PC	58.8%	56.2%
LIB	22.1%	30.0%
NDP	16.8%	11.7%
IND	—	1.9%
CONFED RWP	1.6%	—
GREEN	.7%	—
M-L	—	.2%
TOTAL	43,799	33,307
LETHBRIDGE-FOOTHILLS	**1984**	**1980**
PC	67.4%	68.6%
LIB	11.4%	17.3%
NDP	14.7%	10.0%
NO AFFILIATION	4.6%	1.2%
SC	1.0%	2.6%
CONFED RWP	.9%	—
COMM	—	.3%
TOTAL	46,480	39,808
MEDICINE HAT	**1984**	**1980**
PC	75.8%	70.3%
LIB	9.0%	17.5%
NDP	10.4%	9.4%
CONFED RWP	3.2%	—
SC	1.7%	2.8%
TOTAL	44,854	36,845
PEACE RIVER	**1984**	**1980**
PC	62.2%	59.4%
LIB	13.2%	19.6%
NDP	15.4%	17.0%
CONFED RWP	7.0%	—
RHINO	—	1.7%
GREEN	1.4%	—
SC	.9%	1.5%
IND	—	.9%
TOTAL	41,209	31,932
PEMBINA	**1984**	**1980**
PC	70.6%	64.7%
LIB	11.6%	23.6%
NDP	15.7%	10.8%
CONFED RWP	2.0%	—
SC	—	1.0%
COMM	.2%	—
TOTAL	62,388	48,679
RED DEER	**1984**	**1980**
PC	75.4%	74.8%
LIB	9.4%	14.6%
NDP	9.4%	7.9%
CONFED RWP	4.5%	—
SC	1.3%	2.8%
TOTAL	55,276	42,486

CONSTITUENCY RESULTS	1984	1980
VEGREVILLE	**1984**	**1980**
PC	80.2%	74.8%
LIB	6.9%	12.7%
NDP	9.4%	9.2%
CONFED RWP	1.3%	—
SC	.9%	1.7%
RHINO	.9%	1.1%
COMM	.5%	.5%
TOTAL	40,498	34,331
WETASKIWIN	**1984**	**1980**
PC	70.9%	75.0%
LIB	7.6%	14.7%
NDP	13.2%	10.4%
CONFED RWP	7.2%	—
SC	1.1%	—
TOTAL	42,474	35,501
YELLOWHEAD	**1984**	**1980**
PC	74.0%	69.5%
LIB	8.1%	18.2%
NDP	13.6%	11.3%
CONFED RWP	1.6%	—
RHINO	1.5%	—
SC	1.1%	—
IND	—	.6%
IND	—	.4%
TOTAL	50,620	40,236
NEWFOUNDLAND		
BONAVISTA-TRINITY-CONCEPTION	**1984**	**1980**
PC	55.0%	30.2%
LIB	40.8%	52.1%
NDP	4.1%	16.6%
NO AFFILIATION	—	1.1%
TOTAL	34,550	27,776
BURIN-ST. GEORGE'S	**1984**	**1980**
PC	47.4%	16.4%
LIB	46.3%	69.9%
NDP	6.4%	13.7%
TOTAL	27,836	21,430
GANDER-TWILLINGATE	**1984**	**1980**
PC	43.1%	28.2%
LIB	53.1%	63.3%
NDP	3.8%	8.5%
TOTAL	30,314	27,591
GRAND FALLS-WHITEBAY-LABRADOR	**1984**	**1980**
PC	42.3%	25.0%
LIB	45.1%	52.7%
NDP	12.6%	22.3%
TOTAL	28,668	29,487

CONSTITUENCY RESULTS	1984	1980
HUMBER-PORT AU PORT-ST.BARBE	1984	1980
PC	46.9%	23.2%
LIB	48.3%	44.6%
NDP	4.2%	32.3%
IND	.5%	—
TOTAL	36,051	29,557
ST. JOHN'S EAST	1984	1980
PC	78.3%	61.3%
LIB	14.3%	25.5%
NDP	6.6%	12.2%
LIBERT	.8%	—
IND	—	.8%
M-L	—	.3%
TOTAL	39,419	32,661
ST. JOHN'S WEST	1984	1980
PC	76.0%	55.2%
LIB	19.6%	33.1%
NDP	4.4%	11.5%
M-L	—	.3%
TOTAL	44,321	34,543

CONSTITUENCY RESULTS	1984	1980
YUKON TERRITORY-YUKON	1984	1980
PC	56.8%	40.6%
LIB	21.7%	39.6%
NDP	16.1%	19.8%
LIBERT	4.4%	—
RHINO	1.1%	—
TOTAL	11,704	9,669
NORTHWEST TERRITORIES NUNATSIAQ	1984	1980
PC	32.5%	7.8%
LIB	28.9%	41.8%
NDP	28.7%	47.3%
IND	10.0%	—
RHINO	—	3.2%
TOTAL	6,886	5,687
WESTERN ARCTIC	1984	1980
PC	46.1%	33.8%
LIB	25.9%	ô2.6%
NDP	28.0%	33.6%
TOTAL	12,624	10,518

* REPORT OF THE CHIEF ELECTORAL OFFICER
NOTE: NUMBERS MAY NOT ADD UP TO 100 DUE TO ROUNDING.

75

108

843